USA

THE LAND WITH AT LEAST 50 OPTIONS

A Hilarious and Eye-Opening Tour of America's
States, One Grocery Aisle at a Time

ROBERT OKINE

USA The Land with At Least 50 Options™

A Hilarious and Eye-Opening Tour of America's States, One Grocery Aisle at a Time

Published by Fifty Options Press™

USA The Land with At Least 50 Options™ is a trademark of Robert Okine and is part of a nonfiction series exploring a variety of cultural and lifestyle topics across the 50 United States.

This is a work of humor and cultural commentary. While it draws inspiration from real places and general observations, all content is original, created for entertainment and insight. Any resemblance to actual grocery store layouts, brand choices, or shopping behaviors is deliciously coincidental.

Cover design, layout, and formatting by Robert Okine and creative collaborators using AI-assisted tools.

Published in the United States of America.

First Edition, 2025

For information, collaborations, or speaking inquiries, visit

www.therobertokine.com

A Hilarious and Eye-Opening Tour of America's States, One Grocery Aisle at a Time

DEDICATION

To my family—Yaanieta, Jason, and Kaitlyn— the ones who've filled every trip with love, laughter, and curiosity.

Thank you for being my favorite travel companions, my everyday joy, and my reason for turning every grocery aisle—no matter the country—into a shared adventure.

This book is for you,
with love and cartfuls of gratitude.

— Robert

ACKNOWLEDGMENTS

Writing this book has been one of the most unexpectedly joyful adventures of my life—and like all great journeys, I didn't travel it alone.

To my incredible wife, **Yaanieta**, and our amazing children, **Jason and Kaitlyn**—thank you for being my inspiration, my grounding force, and my greatest source of laughter and love. Our shared travels and global grocery runs made this book possible. Every aisle, every snack, every discovery—it all began with you.

To my wider family and friends across the world, thank you for cheering me on, feeding my curiosity, and always asking *what's next*. Your support gave me the confidence to believe that this quirky idea could become a real book.

And finally, to every reader who's picked this up—thank you. I hope you smile, laugh, nod in recognition, and maybe even wander your local grocery store with fresh eyes. America has at least 50 options... and now you've seen them all.

With deepest gratitude,
Robert Okine

PREFACE: AISLES OF AMERICA

Welcome to the most delicious road trip you never expected.

This book isn't about the best restaurants in America. It's not about gourmet chefs, Michelin stars, or 17-course tasting menus with foam.

It's about **grocery stores.**

The humble, beautiful, chaotic places where *real food meets real life*. Where culture, comfort, convenience, and chaos all live under fluorescent lights.

From crab cakes in Maryland to chili dogs in Michigan... from maple syrup in Vermont to poke bowls in Hawaii... Every grocery store tells a story—**and every cart has a personality.**

As a global nomad turned grocery philosopher, I stepped into American stores like an anthropologist with a shopping list. And what I found?

Flavor. Identity. Humor. Pride. Confusion. And aisles of *so many options* I nearly lost my mind in the almond milk section.

This book is my love letter to America—one grocery cart at a time.

Welcome to *USA: The Land with at Least 50 Options*. Now grab a cart. Let's shop the country.

– Robert Okine

TABLE OF CONTENTS

WELCOME TO THE LAND OF CHOICE OVERLOAD

W hen I first moved to the United States, I expected culture shock. I expected fast food on every corner, big cars, friendly strangers, and maybe even a little cowboy music. What I didn't expect was standing frozen in a grocery store aisle—staring at *fifty kinds of bread.*

White bread. Wheat bread. Gluten-free. Keto-friendly. Low-carb. Sprouted. With seeds. Without seeds. With oats. With *ancient* grains.

All I wanted was something to make a sandwich.

That moment, standing in front of a wall of bread like it was the Sistine Chapel, was when it hit me:

The United States of America isn't just the land of opportunity. It's the land of options.

Not just in grocery stores, but in life itself.

Everywhere you go—every state, every city—you're surrounded by choice.

Where to live. What to eat. What to believe. What to wear. Who to be.

It's incredible. It's overwhelming. It's hilarious. It's profound.

And it's very, *very* American.

This book is my way of celebrating (and gently poking fun at) this beautiful, bold buffet of choices. I take you through all 50 states, one at a time, uncovering a quirky side of American life—often through what you find in a simple store aisle.

Because in a country where your almond milk can be unsweetened, vanilla-flavored, calcium-enriched, and locally sourced...

You better believe every state's got a story.

Welcome to the Land of At Least 50 Options.

Let's explore.

CHAPTER 1

CALIFORNIA–AVOCADO EVERYTHING & ALMOND MILK DECISIONS

When people think of California, they picture sunshine, palm trees, and actors pretending not to be actors. What they don't always picture is the mental gymnastics it takes to pick a carton of milk.

Welcome to California, where even *your choices have choices*.

Aisle 7: Existential Crisis

My first time in a California grocery store, I stood in front of the milk section for thirteen minutes. I timed it.

Almond milk, oat milk, rice milk, soy milk, cashew milk, macadamia milk, banana milk (yes, banana), goat milk, A2 cow milk, raw milk, coconut milk, hemp milk... and one sad little carton of actual whole milk trying not to get canceled.

And that's before you get to the options:

- Sweetened or unsweetened?
- Vanilla or original?
- Fortified with calcium, vitamin D, or turmeric?
- "Barista blend," "Keto-friendly," or "Mood-enhancing"?

At some point I forgot I came for cereal.

The Culture of Clean Eating

California doesn't just want you to eat healthy—it wants you to *feel enlightened* while doing it. You can get quinoa that's been blessed by a yoga instructor. Granola that's 87% chia seeds and 13% well-meaning intentions. Kombucha brewed in small batches by monks—or maybe just guys with man buns in Oakland.

Every store here smells like essential oils, ambition, and fresh basil. There's a Whole Foods across from a Sprouts next to a Trader Joe's that shares a parking lot with a juice cleanse pop-up.

Even the dogs eat organic.

The Vibe is Wellness Meets Wealth

Everyone is either on a cleanse, intermittent fasting, or drinking something green in a mason jar.

And you don't just buy groceries—you **curate** them.

You don't say "I picked up snacks." You say, "I discovered these almond flour seaweed crisps at this boutique vegan co-op in Santa Monica. They're life-changing."

Life-changing.

Meanwhile, I'm just trying to find bread that isn't gluten-intolerant.

The Abundance Paradox

It's incredible, though. In one place, you can choose food that fits any identity:

- Vegan? Got you.
- Paleo-Keto-CrossFit-Carnivore? Yup.
- Anti-carb but pro-cookie? There's a "keto cookie butter" option with a cult following.

California gives you everything. And then it gives you another option, just in case.

Final Thought

In California, you don't just choose what you eat.

You choose *who you are* based on what you put in your cart.

So next time you're in LA and someone asks what your sign is, don't say *Capricorn.*

Say *Oat Milk Rising.*

CHAPTER 2
NEW YORK–SO MANY OPTIONS, SO LITTLE TIME

New York City doesn't sleep. It *barely blinks*. And neither do its grocery stores. In fact, some of them are open 24/7—not because people need groceries at 3 a.m., but because *someone might*.

In a city where space is tight, time is money, and everyone's in a hurry, you'd think the choices would be limited. Spoiler: **they are not**.

Welcome to the 24-Hour Gourmet Gauntlet

Imagine a deli the size of a walk-in closet. Now imagine it offering:

- Korean kimchi
- Jamaican patties
- Organic kefir
- Six kinds of Greek yogurt

- A hot buffet with sushi, lasagna, and oxtail stew
- Oh, and a tiny flower stand squeezed in for good measure

It's as if every culture in the world had a potluck—and left their leftovers in your corner bodega.

The Bodega Ballet

Every New Yorker has a favorite bodega. Not because it's the closest. Not because it's the cheapest. But because *they know your sandwich order by heart.*

You walk in, nod once, and ten minutes later—without a word—your toasted everything bagel with scallion cream cheese, turkey bacon, and a splash of hot sauce appears in a brown paper bag like magic.

They don't call it "service."

They call it **Tuesday.**

Whole Foods or Whole Paycheck

Then there's Whole Foods—the cathedral of clean eating—where a cucumber costs more than a taxi ride.

And yet, New Yorkers flock there, because:

1. It's air-conditioned
2. It has free samples

3. It's one of the few places where you can find celery juice, pasture-raised duck eggs, and gluten-free ravioli—all in one aisle.

And if that's not enough, you can hit Trader Joe's afterward for a frozen butter chicken and a bottle of $2 wine with a French name.

Because options.

Speed Meets Excess

Here's the irony: **New Yorkers are in a rush, but their groceries take forever to choose.**

Why? Because the city gives you:

- 13 salad dressings
- 6 hummus flavors
- 9 types of sparkling water
- A nervous breakdown in aisle 3

And if you can't find what you want? No problem. The guy behind you in line will loudly suggest it, *then buy it first.*

Final Thought

In New York, your groceries say more about you than your resume.

You are:

- **Trader Joe's and chill**? Brooklyn.
- **Whole Foods and oat milk**? Manhattan.
- **Bodega sandwich with Arizona Iced Tea**? Bronx legend.

So go ahead—grab your overpriced celery juice and your vegan mango seaweed jerky.

And keep moving. You're holding up the line.

CHAPTER 3

TEXAS – GO BIG OR BUY BIGGER

Everything's bigger in Texas. The trucks. The hats. The pride.

And, most importantly, the **grocery carts.**

I'm not talking about the normal little metal baskets you find in your average store. No—Texas carts are engineered for survival. You could stack them with three watermelons, a toddler, two briskets, and still have room for a six-pack of jalapeño root beer.

Aisle 14: Brisket, Beans, and Barbecue Belief Systems

Texans don't just buy food.

They **believe** in it.

Barbecue in Texas isn't a dish—it's a philosophy. You don't choose a barbecue sauce. You pledge allegiance to it.

And if you dare pick up a bottle labeled "Carolina Style," be ready for a full-blown intervention.

"Bless your heart," they'll say, politely.

Which in Texas... means exactly the opposite.

The Religion of Ranch Dressing

One time in Dallas, I found an entire shelf dedicated to ranch dressing. Not the usual bottle or two—**a whole shrine**.

You had:

- Classic Ranch
- Spicy Ranch
- Bacon Ranch
- Avocado Ranch
- "Cool Ranch" that suspiciously looked like Doritos in a bottle

I counted 17 ranch varieties. And that's before we get to the *Ranch-inspired dips* and *Ranch-flavored chips*.

At some point, I began to question: **Am I inside a store, or a ranch dressing museum?**

Texas Is for Carnivores (and Then Some)

The meat section in Texas is bigger than most New York apartments.

You can get:

- Smoked turkey legs the size of a toddler's thigh
- Five-pound packs of bacon
- Steak so big it comes with a warning label

And of course—brisket. Sold pre-cooked, slow-cooked, flash-frozen, or vacuum-sealed in holy BBQ sauce.

Vegetarians, beware. Even the salads here come with bacon and judgment.

Bulk Buying Like a Boss

Texans love a good deal—and a good bulk.

Why buy one when you can buy **twelve and freeze them for the apocalypse**?

- 3-gallon jars of pickles
- 24-packs of root beer
- Cheese wheels the size of spare tires
- Enough paper towels to clean up after an oil spill

And don't forget the aisle with 50-pound bags of dog food—for your Chihuahua.

Final Thought

In Texas, **small is suspicious**.

You don't walk into a store for *just one item*. You walk in like you're preparing for a family reunion, a rodeo, and a power outage—all at once.

So if you ever find yourself in a Texas grocery store wondering whether to buy the 3-pound brisket or the 12-pound one...

Just remember:

Go big or bless your heart.

CHAPTER 4

HAWAII–SPAM, SEAWEED & SUNSET SNACKS

L anding in Hawaii feels like stepping into a postcard. Turquoise waves. Warm breezes. Friendly shakas.

And in the grocery store?

Spam for days.

Yes, Spam. The canned meat. The icon. The Hawaiian MVP.

Spam is a Love Language

In Hawaii, Spam is *not* a joke.

It's lunch.

It's love.

It's legacy.

There's even a local dish called **Spam musubi**—a slice of

grilled Spam on a block of rice, wrapped in seaweed like sushi's laid-back cousin.

You'll find it in gas stations, high-end restaurants, your auntie's fridge, and yes—every aisle of every store.

There are flavors I'd never imagined existed:

- Spam Teriyaki
- Spam Jalapeño
- Spam Tocino
- Spam Lite (for when you care, but not that much)

I stood in awe. A whole shelf... no, **an altar**... dedicated to processed pork.

Grocery Shopping as a Cultural Tour

Hawaiian grocery stores are like edible history museums.

You'll see:

- Portuguese sweet bread
- Japanese mochi
- Filipino lumpia wrappers
- Hawaiian poke in 6 flavors
- Taro chips, passionfruit syrup, and guava everything

It's a beautiful blend—just like Hawaii itself.

And the best part? Everyone seems cool with it. Like, "Yeah, we eat rice with everything. You should too."

The Price Tag Shock

Ah, yes. Then there's the small matter of... pricing.

Because when you live on an island, things arrive by boat or by miracle.

So don't be surprised when:

- A gallon of milk costs $8
- A pineapple is cheaper than a bag of Doritos
- You rethink your life decisions in the frozen aisle

Basically, if you're coming from the mainland, you'll feel like your grocery bill went to Disneyland without you.

Island Health Vibes

Hawaii also has that breezy, healthy-living energy:

- Coconut water in every form (raw, cold-pressed, sparkling)
- Macadamia nut snacks with five ingredients—and five syllables each
- Protein bars that sound like surfboard brands

Even the soda aisle has kombucha wearing flip-flops.

Final Thought

In Hawaii, food is more than fuel.

It's a fusion of cultures, a celebration of nature, and a love letter wrapped in seaweed.

And whether you're eating Spam musubi on a beach or sipping coconut milk with a view of the sunset...

You're reminded that *paradise tastes better with options.*

CHAPTER 5

FLORIDA–CHAOS, SUNSHINE, AND 37 TYPES OF ORANGE JUICE

F lorida is America's wildcard.

It's where retirees, spring breakers, and iguanas falling from trees all somehow coexist.

It's where a shopping cart might contain kale, gator jerky, sunscreen, and a full beach chair—because **Florida lives in the moment.**

And if that moment includes orange juice?

You have 37 ways to say yes.

Aisle 2: Orange Juice Olympics

In Florida, the juice aisle isn't an aisle—it's a *festival.*

You've got:

- Pulp

- No pulp
- Some pulp
- Calcium added
- Vitamin D enhanced
- "Freshly Squeezed"
- "Not From Concentrate"
- "Made With Real Florida Sunshine" (I don't even know what that means)

There's OJ with mango.

OJ with turmeric.

OJ with probiotics.

OJ for kids.

OJ for "active lifestyles."

OJ for "active kids with probiotics and mango."

I stood there wondering:

Should I hydrate... or call my therapist?

The Florida Shopping Experience

Shopping in Florida is never boring. You may witness:

- A man in swim trunks and flip-flops buying pool noodles and beef jerky
- Someone arguing with a parrot on their shoulder
- A person trying to return a half-eaten papaya while sipping wine from a can (yes, that happened)

It's not just a grocery run.

It's *live theater*.

Publix: The Local Religion

Floridians take their supermarket loyalty *very* seriously.

Enter: **Publix**—the sacred temple of subs, sales, and smiles.

The "Pub Sub" (Publix submarine sandwich) is a **cultural phenomenon**.

There are Facebook groups.

There are Reddit threads.

There are weddings that have probably included a tray of chicken tender subs.

You don't question the Pub Sub. You *respect* the Pub Sub.

Tropical Temptations

Beyond the chaos, Florida is a tropical produce paradise:

- Mangoes the size of your head
- Guava, lychee, passionfruit
- Key limes and key lime pie *in frozen, baked, and powdered form*

- Papayas that look like they're training for a wrestling match

Even the pineapples seem to smile here.

Final Thought

In Florida, the grocery store reflects the state itself: wild, sunny, unpredictable, and full of flavor.

And while you might walk in for one thing and come out with a beach umbrella, coconut body wash, and three types of OJ...

You won't regret a thing.

Because in Florida, the only rule is:

Stay hydrated and enjoy the chaos.

CHAPTER 6

OREGON – HIPSTER AISLES AND HEMP MILK HYPE

Ah, Oregon. The land of misty mornings, mossy forests, and people who forage for mushrooms *because they want to*, not because they have to.

Walk into a grocery store here, and you'll quickly realize: You're not shopping.

You're **curating your identity**—one ethically sourced, low-carbon, gluten-free product at a time.

The Grocery Vibe: Quirky, Quietly Judging

In Oregon, grocery stores whisper:

"Are you buying that... consciously?"

You'll find:

- Seven types of oat milk

- Three types of hemp milk
- Flax milk, pea milk, walnut milk
- And something called "mylk" that legally isn't allowed near cows

One time, I picked up "activated charcoal coconut kefir water," and the label literally said:

"Best enjoyed under moonlight."

I didn't question it. I just nodded respectfully.

Bulk Bins & BYOJ (Bring Your Own Jar)

In Portland, they don't just encourage recycling. They **expect** it.

Forget plastic. Forget pre-packaged.

You bring your jars, your cloth bags, maybe even a reusable scoop made from bamboo and dreams.

The bulk bin section is a *philosophy*.

Lentils, quinoa, chia seeds, cacao nibs, dried hibiscus petals... It's like a make-your-own trail mix bar for enlightened hikers.

You'll overhear phrases like:

- "These goji berries are local."
- "I just can't support turmeric that's flown in."
- "Did you hear they ethically compost their compost?"

The Kombucha Conundrum

Kombucha is not a trend in Oregon. It's a **lifestyle**.

Whole aisles are dedicated to the fizzy, fermented, slightly suspicious beverage that tastes like vinegar married a peach and they had fizzy, probiotic babies.

Flavors I've seen:

- Hibiscus Lavender Reishi
- Ginger Turmeric Honeybee
- Pineapple Cayenne Enlightenment
- "Mystic Mango" (may cause spiritual visions)

I once accidentally bought a kombucha labeled "Spiritual Cleanse."

It cleaned me out in ways I'm still processing.

Guilt-Free Everything

Every product in Oregon has a label. But not just nutritional info—no, we're talking:

- Certified regenerative
- Cruelty-free
- Zero-waste
- Fair-trade
- Locally sourced
- Made by left-handed artists on a bike-powered machine

And still, somehow, it tastes like air and ambition.

Final Thought

Oregon grocery stores don't just feed you—they *challenge* you.

To think deeper. Shop better. And maybe even compost your soul.

Because in Oregon, choosing between five kinds of eco-friendly granola isn't overwhelming.

It's a **moral responsibility**.

CHAPTER 7

WISCONSIN–CHEESE AISLE ROYALTY

f America had a royal family, Wisconsin would be the dairy queen.

This is not a state that merely *likes* cheese.

This is a state that **crowns it**, worships it, and possibly names its children after it.

Walk into a Wisconsin grocery store and brace yourself.

You are now entering the **cheese zone**.

Aisle 5: Glory, Glory, Haloumi

The cheese aisle isn't an aisle.

It's a **cathedral** of cheddar.

Blocks, slices, wedges, curds, spreads.

Cheese in tubs, sticks, bricks, wheels, sprays (we forgive them for that last one).

Mild cheddar. Sharp cheddar. Extra sharp cheddar.

"Don't look it in the eye" cheddar.

And don't you dare forget:

- Colby Jack
- Havarti with dill
- Smoked gouda
- Fresh mozzarella balls swimming in olive oil like lazy spa guests

I saw a cheese shaped like the state of Wisconsin.

I cried.

Curd Culture

If you've never had a fresh Wisconsin cheese curd, don't say "cheese lover" around here.

It's like walking into Paris and asking where the best microwaved croissants are.

Curds are squeaky, bouncy, salty little miracles.

They sell them:

- Plain
- Battered and fried
- Spicy
- Beer-battered

- In gift baskets labeled *"Curd Your Enthusiasm"*

You haven't lived until you've had curds warm from the fryer in a grocery deli next to a guy wearing a Packers jersey and snow boots in July.

Sausage Sidekicks

Right beside the cheese shrine is the **sausage support group**.

Brats, summer sausage, pepperoni sticks, beef jerky bouquets.

Some of them come with cheese already *inside*—because why separate soulmates?

It's not just protein.

It's a lifestyle snack.

Cold Weather = Cozy Carts

Winter in Wisconsin means grocery stores transform into **survival hubs**:

- Giant bags of shredded cheese
- Hot cocoa in industrial drums
- Frozen casseroles with names like "Grandma's Revenge"

- And entire shelves dedicated to *seven-layer dip kits* for Sunday football

Every shopping trip feels like you're stocking up for a blizzard, even if it's 68 degrees.

Final Thought

In Wisconsin, cheese isn't just food.

It's a love language, a regional identity, and a way of life.

And if you walk out of a grocery store without at least *three* cheeses and something smoked in your bag?

Well, you're probably just passing through.

CHAPTER 8

IOWA—CORNFIELDS, CASSEROLES & CEREAL AISLE SHOCK

Welcome to Iowa—the calm, quiet heart of America. It's where your neighbors wave, your casseroles have names, and the corn stretches farther than your cell signal.

But don't let the peaceful vibe fool you.

Inside the grocery store, **you will face the most overwhelming cereal aisle of your life.**

Aisle 3: Cereal, Sweet Cereal, and Existential Crisis

Iowa is home to **General Mills and Quaker Oats**. That means the cereal aisle here is not just big—it's *epic*.

We're talking:

- Frosted

- Flavored
- Fruity
- Fiber-rich
- Chocolatey
- High-protein
- Gluten-free
- Mini wheats, big flakes, honey clusters, mystery shapes

And don't forget:

- Cereal straws
- Cereal bars
- Cereal-infused protein shakes
- Limited-edition cereals named after cartoon characters no one remembers

I counted **62 cereal options** once. And that's not including oatmeal, which has its *own section*—flavored like everything from apples to ambition.

Corn in All the Ways

In Iowa, corn isn't just a side dish. It's the **main character**.

You'll find:

- Cornmeal
- Cornbread mix
- Corn chips
- Corn pasta
- Corn syrup in half your pantry

- Popcorn in every flavor from cheddar to birthday cake

And somewhere in the freezer section: corn dogs wearing tiny jackets of nostalgia.

If you haven't tried deep-fried corn on a stick at a grocery deli in Des Moines, have you even lived?

Casserole Central

Midwestern groceries in Iowa lean heavy into *comfort food.*

Frozen section? Full of lasagnas, chicken pot pies, beefy stews, and mysterious creations with tater tots on top.

Locals don't say "casserole." They say **hot dish**, and serve it with pride and possibly a side of jello salad.

If you ask what's in it, the answer is usually:

"You'll like it."

(You will.)

Polite Prices and Politer People

Iowa grocery stores are affordable, friendly, and full of employees who might know your cousin.

You'll hear:

- "Oh hey, didn't I see you at the tractor pull?"
- "Your usual brand of peanut butter's on sale, hon."
- "Careful now, it's slippery by the frozen peas."

And that's not customer service.

That's **community**.

Final Thought

In Iowa, you may walk into a grocery store thinking you know cereal.

But you'll walk out questioning everything—except whether you're buying a family-sized lasagna tonight.

Because in Iowa, **food is love**, and they serve it in generous portions.

CHAPTER 9

MONTANA – BIG SKY, BIG STEAKS, BIGGER FREEZERS

M ontana isn't just a state—it's a *state of mind.*

One part cowboy grit, one part mountain serenity, and one part "I-hunt-my-own-dinner."

In the grocery store, this translates into two truths:

1. **Meat is king.**
2. **Freezer space is sacred.**

Aisle 12: The Great Wall of Meat

Montana's meat section isn't "well-stocked."

It's **armed**.

You'll find:

- Elk sausage
- Bison patties

- Venison jerky
- Steaks with marbling so beautiful it should be framed

And don't be surprised if someone next to you says,

"Oh, I shot one just like that last season."

This isn't "farm to table."

This is **field to freezer**, sometimes with a taxidermy detour in between.

The Freezer is Your Friend

In Montana, people **prepare**.

Winters are long. Grocery runs are *rare*. And having enough frozen food is a **social responsibility.**

There are chest freezers in garages.

Basement freezers.

Freezers inside other freezers.

Some homes even have "meat rooms"—which are exactly what they sound like.

At the store, you'll see:

- Bulk packs of ground beef (10 lbs minimum)
- Full racks of ribs
- Family lasagnas the size of doormats
- Frozen burritos sold in *sleeping bag quantities*

DIY Aisles & Rugged Rations

Montanans are the original DIYers.

- Bread mix? Check.
- Canning jars? Always.
- Dehydrated soup pouches for your next backpacking trip through bear country? You bet.

Even the spice aisle feels like a nod to self-reliance: "Make your own rubs," it says. "Be a pioneer."

And somewhere near the trail mix, you'll find **bear spray**. Because Montana.

Quiet Carts, Strong Opinions

People in Montana don't say much while shopping. But they notice.

They see what brand of coffee you buy.

They nod at your jerky selection.

They judge silently if you buy "city eggs."

The cashier might not say much either, but their "Have a good one" carries the weight of the mountains.

Final Thought

Montana grocery shopping is not for the faint-hearted.

It's for the **prepared, the practical, and the protein-powered.**

And if you ever feel overwhelmed by all the beef options...

Just ask yourself:

"What would a grizzly eat?"

Then get the double pack.

CHAPTER 10

UTAH–CEREAL WALLS AND FAMILY-SIZED EVERYTHING

Welcome to Utah, where the mountains are majestic, the families are large, and the grocery carts? **Extra wide.**

Shopping here isn't just a chore—it's a strategy.

Because when you've got **six kids, a dog, and a neighbor you're secretly cooking for**, you don't buy snacks.

You buy **snack ecosystems.**

Aisle 4: The Cereal Colosseum

Utah is *cereal country.*

 Not just because people love breakfast. But because cereal is **a pantry staple, dessert, snack, bribe, and ice cream topping.**

In one aisle, I saw:

- Lucky Charms, in 3 different box sizes
- Frosted Mini-Wheats, now with *blessed cinnamon*
- "Crispy Rice"—Utah's kind, devout cousin of Rice Krispies
- Generic brands with names like "Magic Stars," "Toasty Flakes," and "Honey Oh Rounds"

And then I saw the **family-size cereal box**—more like *family tower*.

You could build a playhouse out of it.

The Cart is Your Kingdom

Forget handheld baskets.

Utah carts are like **SUVs with wheels.**

Some stores even have double-decker carts to accommodate:

- 3 gallons of milk
- 48 eggs
- A six-pack of peanut butter
- One child seated, another standing, a third possibly riding the undercarriage

I once watched a woman push two full carts while answering a call, sipping a green smoothie, and singing to her baby.

That's not grocery shopping.

That's **aerobic multitasking.**

The Rise of "Prepared but Pure"

Utah shoppers love ready-to-go foods—but **clean** ones.

No preservatives, thank you. But sure, throw in:

- Organic pancake mix
- Sugar-free elderberry syrup
- Vegan bacon made from yams and prayers

Even the frozen pizza aisle has options like:

- "Non-GMO Garden Delight"
- "Celestial Crust with Goat Cheese & Gratitude"

Bulk is the Baseline

In Utah, **bulk isn't a category—it's a religion.**

This is home to Costco megachurches and pantry shelves so well-stocked they might qualify as emergency bunkers.

Need flour?

You can get it by the bag, bucket, or barrel.

Crackers?

There's a "variety box" so big, it has a **handle**.

Cookies?

Yes, but please choose from *three dozen-count trays*, individually sealed for freshness and righteousness.

Final Thought

In Utah, grocery shopping is about two things:

feeding many and feeding them well.

It's clean. It's efficient. It's *immaculately organized.*

And if you're ever unsure what to buy, look for the cereal tower with the most smiling children on the box.

That's the one.

CHAPTER 11:

LOUISIANA – CREOLE, CAJUN & CRAWFISH CHOICES

n Louisiana, flavor doesn't whisper.

It **sings**, it shimmies, it kicks down the door wearing hot sauce earrings.

Whether you're in New Orleans or a sleepy bayou town, a trip to the grocery store is more than shopping—it's a **parade of spice, soul, and seasoning.**

Aisle 8: The Holy Trinity of Louisiana Cooking

First thing you notice?

The spice section is longer than the frozen food aisle.

We're talking:

- Cajun seasoning

- Creole seasoning
- Blackened this, smoked that
- "Slap Ya Mama" (Yes, it's a real brand. No, don't slap your mama.)
- Hot sauces in bottles shaped like skulls, gators, and jazz trumpets

And every shelf seems to whisper:

"Whatever you're cooking, add more flavor."

Gumbo Kits & Crawfish Dreams

In Louisiana, **gumbo is a birthright**.

It's not "soup"—it's a slow-cooked spiritual experience.

You'll find:

- Roux in jars
- Gumbo bases
- Okra by the pound
- Sausage smoked with ancient secrets
- Crawfish tails frozen, fresh, peeled, or pickled

Some stores even sell ready-made gumbo, because waiting six hours is fine... but not today.

Rice, Rice, and More Rice

Louisiana has **as many types of rice as Alaska has ice.**

You've got:

- Long-grain
- Medium-grain
- Dirty rice kits
- Red beans and rice mixes
- Jambalaya kits
- Wild rice blend named after someone's grandmother

There's even microwave rice that somehow still slaps.

Boudin, Beignets & Blessings

Walk a few aisles down and suddenly—**bam!**

Boudin sausages. Andouille. Tasso.

Everything smoky, salty, and sassy.

Then you hit the bakery:

- Beignets in boxed mix and frozen packs
- King cake kits (with the baby inside, of course)
- Pralines wrapped in ribbon like they're ready to go to Mardi Gras

Even the bread seems to have attitude.

Jazz in the Aisles

And the people?

They don't rush. They sway.

Someone's grandma might explain why her hot sauce is better than the rest.

The cashier might recommend her uncle's recipe.

And if you're lucky, someone might be humming a blues tune near the catfish filets.

Shopping here is a **mood**.

Final Thought

Louisiana doesn't do bland.

It does **bold, brassy, and blessed with butter**.

And if your cart doesn't smell like spice, seafood, and sweet dough by the time you check out...

Go back.

You missed something.

CHAPTER 12

VERMONT – MAPLE SYRUP AND MINIMALISM

Vermont feels like a deep breath.

Crisp air. Rolling hills. Barns that look like they came with the land.

And in the grocery store? You get the same vibe: **peaceful, purposeful, and probably locally sourced.**

This is where kale goes to rest and maple syrup lives its best life.

Aisle 6: Liquid Gold and Syrup Diplomacy

In Vermont, maple syrup isn't a condiment.

It's a **way of life.**

There's:

- Grade A Amber

- Grade A Dark
- Grade A Very Dark (for serious pancake professionals)
- Organic, raw, barrel-aged, bourbon-barrel-aged
- Syrup infused with vanilla, cinnamon, or *"just Vermont air and vibes"*

Locals have opinions.

Strong ones.

Ask three Vermonters which syrup is best, and you'll spark a quiet but unshakable debate.

And don't even **mention fake syrup**. That's like insulting someone's grandmother to their face.

A Study in Grocery Stillness

No chaos. No carts crashing.

Just gentle nods and shelves that look hand-built.

You'll find:

- Glass bottles instead of plastic
- Hand-labeled jams
- Local cheeses wrapped in wax paper
- Granola with names like "Woodland Crunch" or "Sunrise Bliss"

Even the peanut butter is contemplative.

There's something about shopping here that makes you want to wear wool and start a gratitude journal.

Flannel-Friendly Freezer Section

Even frozen foods here feel handmade:

- Artisan pot pies
- Organic veggie burgers with ingredients like lentils, love, and lichens (probably)
- Locally churned ice cream with flavors like "Maple Apple Crisp" and "Lavender Moon"

Nothing's screaming for your attention.

It just patiently waits.

Cheese with Personality

Don't sleep on the cheese aisle.

Vermont's not just about syrup—it's also home to **world-class cheddar.**

There are wedges aged in caves.

Cheeses named after mountains.

Labels that say things like "sharp enough to challenge your worldview."

Try one, and suddenly you understand why Vermonters walk slower: they're still processing their dairy.

Final Thought

In Vermont, your groceries don't shout.

They speak softly and **mean it.**

You don't rush.

You read the label.

You think about what the cow might've felt.

And you always leave with syrup, cheese, and peace of mind.

CHAPTER 13

ALASKA–FROZEN AISLES & WILD CATCHES

A laska is the kind of place that reminds you: nature always wins.

The mountains are bigger. The air is crisper. The moose are bolder.

And the grocery stores?

They feel like part hardware store, part survival center, part fish market.

Because in Alaska, shopping isn't just about **what you want**—it's about **what might save you later**.

Aisle 11: Welcome to the Deep Freeze

Let's get this out of the way—**everything is frozen.**

There's a special kind of reverence here for:

- Frozen salmon
- Frozen halibut
- Frozen moose meat (yes, moose)
- Frozen reindeer sausage
- Frozen veggies, frozen pies, frozen pancakes, frozen pizza...

- And a freezer chest dedicated solely to **tundra-sized tubs of ice cream**—because apparently, Alaskans eat the most ice cream per capita in the U.S.

Why?

Because if the power goes out, that rocky road becomes **emergency rations**.

Fishing Poles & Flour in the Same Aisle

In Alaska, your grocery store might sell:

- Fresh crab legs
- Organic kale
- Rifles
- Propane tanks
- Scented candles
- A snow shovel
- And a book on surviving bear attacks... all within three aisles.

It's not chaotic. It's **practical**.

Local Catch, Global Prices

The paradox of Alaska: the world's best fish lives here—and yet **your avocado might cost $6.99.**

Because when you live off the mainland, shipping is a game of hope and miracles.

You learn to:

- Appreciate fresh bread like it's gold
- Celebrate when bananas arrive still yellow
- Hoard eggs like you're preparing for the ice age

Grocery trips become **strategic operations**—especially if the weather's about to turn.

Community Fridge Vibes

Despite the remote setting, Alaskan grocery stores feel **surprisingly neighborly**.

It's common to:

- See handwritten notes from local fishermen: *"Try the coho salmon in aisle 2!"*
- Chat with cashiers about glacier melt
- Find a bulletin board near checkout filled with babysitter listings, moose sightings, and hand-carved sleds for sale

This isn't just shopping. It's **staying connected.**

Final Thought

In Alaska, your groceries aren't just food—they're a **lifeline**.

Every can, every frozen bag, every smoked salmon fillet carries weight.

And if you ever feel overwhelmed by the prices or the snow or the moose blocking your car in the parking lot...

 Just grab a pint of ice cream, a bag of jerky, and remind yourself:

You're living where most people only dream of surviving.

CHAPTER 14

NEW JERSEY – PORK ROLL, PRODUCE WARS & DELI DRAMA

N ew Jersey doesn't ask you how your day is.

It tells you how *its* day is going—and then judges your choice of bagels.

And nowhere is this more evident than in the grocery store, where shopping is a contact sport, deli orders are shouted with passion, and **produce is political.**

Aisle 1: Battle of the Bagels

Let's be clear: if you're buying bagels from the bread aisle and not from the fresh bin at the local shop with a name like *"Bagel Boss II,"* people will know.

They will stare.

And they will say something like,

"That's not a real bagel. That's a roll with a hole."

Because in Jersey, bagels aren't breakfast—they're **heritage.**

(And yes, you *do* toast your Taylor ham sandwich. But don't call it "Taylor ham" south of the Raritan River unless you want a full-on cultural debate.)

The Great Pork Roll vs. Taylor Ham Divide

Two words: **Pork. Roll.**

Or... wait. Is it **Taylor Ham**?

Welcome to the most delicious identity crisis in the Northeast.

In North Jersey: *"It's Taylor Ham, bro."*

In South Jersey: *"It's pork roll, and you're wrong."*

And in the grocery store, the packaging tries to play it cool:

"John Taylor's Pork Roll"

Neutral on the outside.

Deeply divisive on the inside.

Deli Counter Dynamics

The deli counter in New Jersey is **a sacred institution.**

It's where:

- Sliced turkey becomes performance art
- Soppressata is pronounced with love
- Orders are shouted over someone else's aunt placing her Thanksgiving catering request in April

The line moves fast, the banter is sharp, and God help you if you forget to take a number.

Also: if your order includes less than a pound of anything, the guy behind you will smirk. *Loudly.*

Produce Stand Politics

Jersey's nickname? The Garden State.

And they **mean it**.

At roadside stands, farmers' markets, and grocery produce sections, you'll find:

- Tomatoes so red they look like they've been in the gym
- Corn on the cob that comes with preparation tips from someone's grandmother
- Peaches, apples, squash—all grown an hour away and sold with pride

But beware: choose the wrong stand, and your neighbor will "gently" suggest a better one.

For the record: their uncle knows a guy. It's fresher. Trust them.

The Grocery Cart Personality Test

In Jersey, your cart tells your story:

- **Entenmann's + cold brew?** Bergen County brunch enthusiast
- **Three bags of rigatoni + five pounds of grated parm?** Nonna's coming over
- **Frozen White Castle burgers + six energy drinks?** You're 23 and your metabolism is still cocky

Judgment is swift.

But also affectionate.

Final Thought

In New Jersey, the grocery store isn't just a store—it's a **mirror of identity, pride, and volume.**

It's loud, it's loyal, and it's **real.**

And if you walk out with pork roll (or Taylor Ham), a dozen bagels, a tomato that smells like August, and a stranger's strong opinion on mozzarella...

You did it right.

CHAPTER 15

NEVADA–JACKPOTS, JERKY & 24-HOUR EVERYTHING

N evada isn't just a place—it's an **energy**.

The kind of energy that says, *"Sure, let's buy sushi at 2 a.m. from a gas station with a slot machine."*

And somehow... it works.

Because in Nevada, **the lights don't go off, and neither do the cravings.**

Aisle 4: Snacks, Sparkles & Sudden Decisions

Walk into any grocery store in Las Vegas and you'll immediately notice:

- Rows of energy drinks
- Neon-colored snacks
- At least three aisles that feel like they were designed by someone pulling an all-nighter in sequins

You can get:

- Flaming hot trail mix
- Wasabi Kit-Kats
- "Hangover Helper" hydration packets
- And bacon-flavored anything (popcorn, toothpaste, spiritual energy bars)

The snack aisle is *chaotic neutral*.

And it loves you.

The 24/7 Grocery Olympics

In Nevada, grocery stores are built for **people with no concept of time**.

You'll see:

- Locals in pajamas buying rotisserie chicken at midnight
- Tourists with glitter in their hair shopping for sunscreen and anxiety meds
- Card dealers grabbing lunch meat and lotto tickets after a 3 a.m. shift

And the staff? Totally unfazed.

"Another guy buying six pints of ice cream and a Sudoku book at 5:42 a.m.?

Cool. Bag or no bag?"

Where Slot Machines Meet Produce

Let's talk about the elephant in the room—or the **slot machine near the restroom**.

Yes, you can gamble inside some grocery stores.

Yes, someone *has* won $40,000 while waiting for their partner to pick a melon.

 And yes, the "jackpot lights" go off right next to the frozen peas.

This is not a drill.

This is **Nevada.**

Desert Survival Meets Indulgence

Nevada grocery stores are a weird and wonderful blend of:

- Essential supplies (water jugs, sunscreen, batteries)
- Party supplies (giant frozen margarita mixes, glow sticks, confetti cannons)
- Gourmet everything (artisan jerky, truffle oil, caviar… at a CVS?)

Even the bottled water section offers a spiritual choice:

- Alkaline
- Ionized
- Reincarnated from glacier tears (allegedly)

Final Thought

In Nevada, grocery shopping is a gamble.

You might walk in for toothpaste and leave with frozen taquitos, a bottle of champagne, and a mild cash prize.

And no one bats an eye.

Because here, **the snack aisle never sleeps.**

CHAPTER 16

IDAHO – POTATOES, PANTRY PRIDE & PRACTICAL MAGIC

I daho is often underestimated.

People hear "Idaho" and think, *"Oh, just potatoes."*

But if you walk into a grocery store here thinking that's all they've got—well, bless your heart and buckle up.

Because in Idaho, the food is **honest, hearty, and surprisingly full of surprises.**

Aisle 5: Potatoes in All Their Glory

Yes, the potato reigns supreme here—and for good reason.

You'll find:

- Russet potatoes
- Yukon Golds
- Fingerlings

- Baby reds
- Pre-cubed, pre-peeled, pre-seasoned
- Mashed, hash-browned, spiralized, frozen, freeze-dried, and in chip form with slogans like *"Made by Idaho sunshine"*

There's even potato **ice cream** somewhere.

Don't ask. Just trust the starch.

Down-to-Earth Shopping Vibes

Idaho grocery stores are **calm, courteous, and wonderfully unpretentious.**

No chaotic crowds. No judgmental glances.

 Just kind faces, wide aisles, and a general sense that someone probably grew the carrots you're buying.

Here, you'll find:

- Jars of apple butter with handwritten labels
- Local honey from bees with better work ethics than most people
- Huckleberry everything—jam, soda, BBQ sauce, probably shampoo too

Even the checkout lane candy feels *wholesome.*

Casserole Country

Frozen section = **comfort food command center**.

Idaho knows how to eat through the winter. You'll see:

- Lasagna as big as your car battery
- Mac & cheese with four types of cheddar
- Chicken pot pie that could feed a town hall meeting
- Meatloaf that comes with a handshake and life advice (probably)

And somewhere in the baking aisle: cream of mushroom soup in **bulk**, because every casserole *needs a co-star*.

Practical, Not Pretentious

This isn't a state obsessed with oat milk or mushroom jerky.

This is a state that says:

"Let's feed the family and still have money for gas."

And they do.

But don't be fooled: behind that practicality is a lot of **pride**.

Local produce. Local ranchers. Local values.

The carrots might have dirt on them—and that's exactly how folks like it.

Final Thought

In Idaho, food is about **feeding people right.**

No gimmicks. No glitz. Just hearty meals, honest prices, and potatoes that could run for mayor.

And if you leave the store without a sack of spuds in your cart?

It's fine.

They'll still wave as you drive by—with a bag ready for next time.

CHAPTER 17

MINNESOTA-TATER TOT HOTDISH & 10,000 KETCHUPS

M innesota is polite, cozy, and colder than your ex's heart in January.

But don't let the quiet charm fool you—when it comes to grocery stores, **Minnesotans don't mess around.**

They shop smart, eat warm, and carry on a proud culinary tradition called **"hotdish"**—basically casserole with *Midwest swagger*.

Aisle 7: Land of 1,000 Cans (and Cream of Mushroom Rules Them All)

Every Minnesotan pantry contains three sacred things:

1. Cream of mushroom soup
2. Frozen green beans

3. Tater tots

Put them together?

Hotdish magic.

In the store, you'll find:

- Shelves dedicated to canned soups
- Tater tots in every shape imaginable
- Pre-shredded cheddar that comes in *snowstorm quantities*
- And "crispy fried onions" that go on *everything* during the holidays (and often... not during the holidays)

Ask for a recipe and someone will say, "Oh, it's just what we always do."

You will never recreate it. Accept that.

The "Minnesota Nice" Grocery Experience

Minnesota shoppers are **absurdly kind**.

They apologize when you bump *them*.

They'll hold a freezer door open for you for ten minutes.

And if you're staring too long at the peanut butter options, someone will softly say:

"Try the natural one. We like it."

Even the employees look like they just finished building a birdhouse for a neighbor.

Ketchup, Jello, and Passive-Aggressive Pasta Salad

You haven't truly shopped in Minnesota until you've seen:

- 14 brands of ketchup
- Jello in boxes, tubs, and possibly **salad form**
- Macaroni salad with mysterious ingredients and a label that just says "Party Size"
- Coleslaw that's aggressively... beige

Is it all good? Yes.

Does it photograph well? Never.

Will you feel loved after eating it? Always.

The Midwestern Freezer Mentality

Minnesotans believe in stocking up.

Winter's coming. And it might stay for six months.

So you'll see:

- Frozen pies stacked like poker chips
- Pancakes in resealable *buckets*
- Casserole kits with names like "Comfort Supreme"
- And an entire aisle of **"bake-and-serve breads"**

in case snow traps you inside and carbs become currency

Final Thought

In Minnesota, grocery shopping isn't flashy.

It's **practical, polite, and powered by community warmth** (and a suspicious amount of mayonnaise).

And if you ever feel unsure what to buy, just ask someone's grandma.

She'll smile, hand you a can of soup, and say:

"Oh honey, just make a hotdish."

CHAPTER 18
NEW MEXICO—RED OR GREEN? YES.

I f you learn one phrase in New Mexico, let it be this:

"Red or green?"

It's not a holiday question. It's a grocery lifestyle. It's a state motto.

It's also a trick question, because the *correct* answer is usually:

"Christmas."

(That's both red and green chile. And yes, it's spelled *chile*, not *chili*. Get it right.)

Aisle 3: The Great Chile Conundrum

In New Mexico, chile isn't a condiment—it's **a cultural identity.**

You'll find:

- Red chile powder, flakes, pastes, sauces, and rubs
- Green chile roasted, diced, jarred, frozen, and *smelling like a religious experience*
- Bags of dried chile pods hanging next to tortillas and tamales
- Local brands with names like "Abuela's Secret Flame" or "Holy Hatch Heat"

Even frozen pizzas have chile on them.

Even jelly.

Even **ice cream.**

(Yes, chile ice cream. Don't knock it.)

Chile Roasting in the Parking Lot

If it's chile season, your grocery store will smell like **heaven and fire had a baby.**

Roasters spin metal drums outside, blasting the air with smoky, spicy perfume that makes you instantly hungry and slightly sweaty.

Locals buy them in **sacks.**

Not bags. Not pounds.

Sacks.

Like they're stocking a bunker for a flavor apocalypse.

Aisle 7: Tortilla Royalty

Tortillas in New Mexico are taken *very seriously.*

There are:

- Flour tortillas
- Corn tortillas
- Blue corn tortillas
- Hatch chile tortillas
- Hand-pressed, stone-ground, blessed-by-Abuelita tortillas

If you buy the wrong brand, someone may kindly correct you.

If you buy *California* tortillas, someone may escort you out.

Beans, Rice, and the Spirit of Slow Simmering

New Mexico groceries honor the holy trinity of:

- Pinto beans
- Spanish rice
- Green chile stew

You'll find:

- Dried beans by the barrel
- Lard that comes in small tubs and giant "I-cook-for-15-people" buckets
- Seasoning packets that say "just add soul" (unironically)

- A slow cooker aisle that feels like a religious shrine

Final Thought

In New Mexico, your grocery cart doesn't just feed your body—it **tells your flavor story.**

Red, green, or Christmas, you're not just shopping.

You're pledging allegiance.

And when you walk out of that store with chile in one hand and tortillas in the other?

You belong.

CHAPTER 19

SOUTH CAROLINA – GRITS, GREENS & GROCERY GOSSIP

I n South Carolina, grocery shopping is an **event.**

You dress a little nicer.

You run into your cousin, your pastor, your ex, and your ex's cousin *within two aisles.*

And by the time you hit the deli, you already know who's getting married, divorced, and who just bought a new riding mower.

Because here, **the grocery store is the heartbeat of the community**—and the fried chicken aisle knows everything.

Aisle 2: Sweet Tea in Gallons & Grace

If you ask someone *"Do y'all have sweet tea?"*

They'll laugh, bless your heart, and point to:

- Gallon jugs
- Mini fridge cartons
- Instant powder mixes
- Glass bottles with *just a splash of lemon and a whole lotta sugar*
- And an entire wall of family recipes… disguised as tea labels

South Carolina runs on **sweet tea and side-eyes.**

Hot Bar Heaven

Forget the salad bar.

In a South Carolina grocery store, you head straight to the **hot bar**, where you'll find:

- Mac and cheese that sticks to your soul
- Fried okra
- Collard greens cooked down *just right*
- Cornbread that makes you rethink everything you knew about flour
- Fried chicken that competes with grandma's (and sometimes wins)

It's not just food—it's **reputation.**

Grits for Days

Grits are more than breakfast here.

They're a canvas.

In the grocery store, you'll find:

- Stone-ground grits
- Instant grits (for the impatient)
- White grits
- Yellow grits
- Shrimp & grits meal kits
- Cheese grits, buttered grits, jalapeño grits
- And a quiet judgment if you say, *"I've never had grits."*

They'll convert you.

Slowly.

With butter.

Cans, Cast Iron, and Casseroles

The South doesn't just believe in feeding people—it believes in **feeding people well.**

So grocery stores carry:

- Canned butter beans and black-eyed peas
- Bacon ends in vacuum-sealed family portions
- Pie crusts that come with recipe tips and a prayer

- "Church dinner starter packs" (not officially labeled, but *you'll know when you see them*)
- And cast iron skillets *in aisle nine,* right next to marshmallows

Because you never know when you'll need to bake a cobbler *and defend your family.*

Final Thought

In South Carolina, a grocery trip is **more than shopping.**

It's community. It's tradition. It's comfort.

And when you leave with a buggy full of sweet tea, fresh biscuits, seasoned greens, and enough gossip to last till Sunday...

You didn't just buy food.

You bought a *moment in the South.*

CHAPTER 20
PENNSYLVANIA-CHEESESTEAKS, PRETZELS & AMISH GOLD

Pennsylvania is a state of contrasts.

You've got the cheesesteak-fueled chaos of Philly, the steel-hearted pride of Pittsburgh, and in between—**Amish country**, where butter comes by the brick and pies are *biblically accurate*.

Shopping here is like flipping between three worlds, and **every single one feeds you well.**

Aisle 6: Pretzel Overload (And We're Not Mad About It)

Pretzels in Pennsylvania are a **food group**.

You'll see:

- Hard pretzels
- Soft pretzels
- Salted, unsalted, honey mustard, sour cream & onion

- Chocolate-covered, peanut butter-stuffed
- Pretzel buns, pretzel nuggets, pretzel sticks that double as weapons

Some bags are so big, they qualify as gym equipment.

And if you *don't* leave with pretzels?

Someone will politely ask if you're feeling okay.

The Holy Cheesesteak Section

Some grocery stores in Philly have **entire setups** for cheesesteak night:

- Thin-sliced ribeye
- Amoroso rolls (anything else is a sin)
- Provolone, Cheez Whiz, or *"wit whiz"*—choose your path
- Hot peppers, fried onions, and just enough grease to call it authentic

The kits even come with instructions, though most locals don't need them.

Because here, cheesesteaks are like lullabies—you grow up on them.

Amish Aisle: Simplicity That Slaps

In Lancaster County and surrounding areas, grocery stores proudly feature **Amish-made products** that put most artisan brands to shame.

You'll find:

- Hand-churned butter that *whispers to your toast*
- Fresh-baked shoofly pie
- Egg noodles so tender they might hug you
- Jars of jam with labels written in cursive (that somehow tastes sweeter)
- Apple butter, chow-chow, pickled everything

The packaging is plain. The flavor is *anything but.*

Snack Supremacy

Pennsylvania doesn't play when it comes to **snacks**.

The chip aisle alone? A masterclass.

You'll see:

- Herr's
- Utz
- Martin's
- BBQ, crab-flavored, sour cream & onion, "Red Hot"
- Giant family-size bags you tell yourself are for sharing (*they're not*)

It's a state where **dipping sauces have their own shelf.**

Ranch. Horseradish. Spicy brown mustard. Mystery "club sauce."

And somehow... it all makes sense.

Final Thought

Pennsylvania grocery stores aren't just about sustenance.

They're about **regional pride served on a plate.**

Whether you're grabbing a cheesesteak kit, loading up on Amish baked goods, or cradling a warm pretzel like it's a newborn...

You'll know exactly where you are.

And you'll never shop the same again.

CHAPTER 21

ARIZONA–HOT SALSA & HYDRATION STATIONS

Arizona is all about extremes.

It's either blazing hot or *oven door left open* hot.

The landscapes are dramatic, the sunsets feel filtered, and the grocery stores?

Let's just say: **when the state is dry, your salsa better not be.**

Aisle 1: The Salsa Situation

Arizona takes its salsas very seriously.

We're talking:

- Roasted chile salsa
- Mango habanero
- Hatch chile verde

- Salsa with pineapple, with corn, with black beans, with ghost peppers, with apologies
- Fresh pico in tubs the size of fishbowls

And chips? **Endless.**

Blue corn, white corn, lime-dusted, cantina-style, cactus-infused.

Some are so crispy, you could hear them crunch from three aisles away.

Here, salsa isn't a topping. It's **a love language.**

The Hydration Olympics

It's hot out. Real hot.

And Arizona grocery stores **prepare you.**

The water aisle is not an aisle—it's a **hydration command center** with:

- Electrolyte water
- Ionized alkaline water
- Cactus water (yes)
- Collagen-infused water
- Water that glows in the dark (okay, probably not, but it *feels* like it)

Also:

- Gatorade in flavors like "Glacier Freeze," "Arctic Blitz," and "Mild Existential Crisis"

- Coconut water with pulp, without pulp, and "vaguely vanilla but not sure why"

Dehydration has no chance here.

Cultural Fusion in Every Aisle

Arizona sits right on the flavor border between American Southwest and Mexican culinary joy.

You'll find:

- Tamale kits
- Tres leches cake in the bakery
- Churro-flavored cereal (yes, it exists)
- Queso dip in jars, tubs, and "family-size survival packs"
- Arizona Iced Tea... *in Arizona*—it's practically a native species

And let's not forget the *Elote aisle* (corn + mayo + cheese = snack royalty).

Frozen Foods That Fight Back

Arizona shoppers know the heat waits for no one—so they stock up on:

- Paletas (Mexican popsicles) in flavors like tamarind and horchata
- Ice cream in tubs the size of car tires

- Frozen burritos, enchiladas, taquitos—because **the oven doesn't have to do all the work**

And don't sleep on the "frozen agua fresca" packets—refreshment, *rebooted*.

Final Thought

In Arizona, groceries reflect the terrain: **hot, bold, and full of unexpected flavor.**

And if your cart has salsa, cactus water, elote chips, and a sun hat you didn't plan to buy...

You're doing it right.

CHAPTER 22

KENTUCKY – BISCUITS, BOURBON & BIZARRE BRAND LOYALTY

Kentucky is soft-spoken, but don't be fooled—it knows exactly what it's doing in the kitchen.

From small-town grocery stores to city markets with country flair, this state brings a mix of **Southern comfort and culinary swagger.**

And yes, that swagger includes an aisle fully dedicated to **cornbread mix** and bourbon-flavored everything.

Aisle 4: Biscuit Brilliance

Let's get one thing straight:

Kentucky knows its biscuits.

You'll find:

- Frozen buttermilk biscuits in family packs

- "Just add water" biscuit mix (which lies—it needs *love*)
- Biscuit flour that somehow smells like Sunday
- Cast iron skillets next to the baking aisle, because presentation matters

There's even biscuit-scented air freshener.

Okay, not really. But... should be.

And if you're buying canned biscuits? Someone's grandma *felt that from a distance.*

The Bourbon Section (No ID Required)

Sure, you've seen wine aisles. But Kentucky grocery stores take **bourbon** seriously—even when it's not alcoholic.

You'll spot:

- Bourbon-infused BBQ sauce
- Bourbon mustard
- Bourbon honey
- Bourbon pecan pie mix
- Bourbon candles
- Bourbon-scented soap (???)

Even the sweet tea here looks like it's been aged in oak barrels.

Meat, Three, and Mystery Casseroles

Grocery delis in Kentucky serve **hot food that deserves its own sitcom**.

You'll see:

- Fried chicken (crispier than common sense)
- Meatloaf slices that whisper "trust me"
- Collard greens with bacon and spiritual depth
- Corn pudding, mac & cheese, and something called "hashbrown casserole," which might be the South's love language

Ask what's in it, and someone will say:

"It's just how we make it."

(Translation: *You'll never know.*)

Canned Food Royalty

Kentucky loves its pantry stock. So yes:

- Black-eyed peas
- Turnip greens
- Pinto beans
- Creamed corn
- Canned peaches swimming in syrup like they're on vacation

And if it comes in a can and ends up in a pie, it's **probably delicious**.

Brand Loyalty with Deep Roots

Some grocery choices are *not* negotiable.

Example:

- **Ale-8-One** soda. You either drink it or you're not from around here.
- **White Lily Flour** for biscuits only.
- **Duke's mayo.** Do *not* show up with anything else.
- Anything else? Optional. These? **Sacred.**

Final Thought

In Kentucky, grocery shopping is a slow stroll through flavor, family, and food wisdom.

If your cart holds biscuit flour, fried chicken, peach preserves, and something with bourbon in it—*even if it's just barbecue sauce...*

You're home.

CHAPTER 23

MASSACHUSETTS–ICED COFFEE IN WINTER & HARVARD IN THE SNACKS

Massachusetts is proud, practical, and perpetually caffeinated.

You'll find Revolutionary War history, Red Sox pride, and people drinking iced coffee during blizzards like it's the most normal thing in the world.

And the grocery store?

It's part brain, part bodega, part **seasonal produce meets seafood empire.**

Aisle 1: The Dunkin' Domination

In Massachusetts, **Dunkin' isn't a coffee chain—it's a lifestyle.**

You'll find:

- Dunkin' coffee beans
- Dunkin' bottled iced coffee
- Dunkin' cereal (yes, that's a thing)
- And an entire section of chilled drinks competing for the title of *Most Likely to Keep You Awake Until 2073*

People don't ask *if* you drink iced coffee in winter.

They ask **what size**.

And if you call it a "frappuccino"?

You might get exiled to Connecticut.

Seafood & Side-Eye

Grocery stores in Massachusetts offer some of the **freshest seafood in the country**, but don't expect warm hugs from the guy at the counter.

You'll get:

- Cod
- Haddock
- Lobster claws the size of your toddler
- Frozen clam chowder "kits" (a.k.a. magic in a bag)
- And oysters that still smell like Cape Cod air

But order slowly and the seafood guy will stare like you just insulted Paul Revere.

Cranberries, Cape Cod Chips & Clam Chowder Kits

Massachusetts grows a *lot* of cranberries—and they make sure you know.

You'll find:

- Cranberry juice, cranberry trail mix, cranberry salsa
- Dried cranberries in every cereal
- Thanksgiving-style cranberry sauce 365 days a year

Plus:

- Cape Cod chips with bags so loud they could wake a Puritan
- Canned chowder next to shucked clams (because *options*)
- Oyster crackers in industrial sizes

It's a snack table *and* a state of mind.

Smart Cart Energy

Massachusetts has a "let's get this done" approach to shopping:

- Read the label. Know the facts. Scan for local.
- Organic is cool, but **New England-sourced** is cooler.
- If it has a story, a founder bio, and a QR code for "traceability"? Sold.

You'll leave with:

- Maple syrup in glass bottles
- Cheese from a place called something like "Happy Cow Hollow"
- And a tote bag that says *Eat Local, Yell Less*

(They never yell less.)

Final Thought

In Massachusetts, your grocery list might say "milk, bread, apples"—but your cart says: **"I'm educated, efficient, and don't mess around with fake clam chowder."**

And if you drink iced coffee with lobster ravioli and cranberry trail mix?

You belong.

CHAPTER 24
NORTH DAKOTA–SNOW PREP, MEAT & MILD SALSA CONFIDENCE

N orth Dakota isn't flashy.

It's **steady, stoic, and deeply practical**—like the friend who brings jumper cables *and* homemade cookies.

And in the grocery store?

It's all about **being ready for anything**—including blizzards, ice storms, and potlucks that pop up out of nowhere.

Aisle 6: Meat Is the Moment

The meat section in North Dakota is **built for the long haul**.

You'll find:

- Ground beef in multi-pound bricks
- Pork chops in economy packs
- Frozen sausage links that could outlive your microwave
- Wild game options, because someone's uncle definitely hunts
- And freezers full of "beef sticks" with names like *Dakota Crunch* or *Prairie Fire*

Meat here isn't just dinner—it's *how you survive February.*

Canned Food Royalty

Let's talk about canned goods.

North Dakotans don't mess around. Their pantries are **legends.**

You'll see:

- Cream of mushroom soup (a hotdish essential)
- Corn, carrots, and green beans in family-stack quantities
- Canned peaches in heavy syrup—dessert or breakfast, *you decide*
- "Mixed vegetables" that no one remembers buying, but always seem to be there

There's a quiet comfort in knowing that *no matter what,* you've got three meals in the cupboard.

Mild Salsa, Maximum Pride

Let's be honest: spice isn't the hero here.

The salsa aisle proudly features:

- Mild
- Extra mild
- "Zesty" (which just means it has onions)
- And a "medium" option that might scare someone's aunt

But what North Dakota lacks in spice, it **makes up for in commitment.**

People here *love* what they love. And they will **defend** their salsa.

Frozen Food Fortress

The freezer section is basically a bunker:

- Family-size lasagna
- Meat pies
- Breakfast sandwiches stacked like ammo
- Giant tubs of vanilla ice cream (no toppings needed, thank you very much)

And don't forget the **boxed dinners**—you haven't lived until you've tried a North Dakota grocery store's "chicken and gravy bake" and thought,

"Why is this... shockingly good?"

Snowstorm Cart Strategy

North Dakotans know how to shop **efficiently**:

- Bread
- Milk
- Eggs
- A roast
- Something sweet (because the storm's coming)
- Something salty (because someone will visit)
- Something frozen (because *you always need something frozen*)

And just like that, they're back in their trucks and home before the wind even howls.

Final Thought

In North Dakota, grocery shopping is about **respecting the weather, the family, and the freezer.**

If your cart holds meat, a few cans of something creamy, and a bag of "zesty" tortilla chips?

You're ready for anything.

Even April.

CHAPTER 25

WASHINGTON – RAIN, ROAST & RECYCLABLES

Washington State is a vibe:

Half Pacific Northwest wonderland, half tech-startup-meets-farmer's-market.

Here, your groceries don't just feed you—they reflect your **values, energy, and carbon footprint.**

And yes, it rains. But somehow... the produce still glows.

Aisle 3: Coffee, Coffee, and More Coffee

You know you're in Washington when:

- The grocery store has a **coffee aisle and a coffee wall**
- Every bag of beans has its *own poetic backstory*
- Labels read like dating profiles:

- *"Single-origin. Mellow. Hints of almond and existential clarity."*

Also:

- Cold brew in glass bottles
- Nitro coffee cans
- Oat milk lattes that cost more than your Wi-Fi

And just outside the store?

A **Starbucks inside a Starbucks**, probably.

The Kombucha Command Center

Washington might as well be the **Napa Valley of kombucha.**

You'll find:

- Lavender lemon kombucha
- Ginger cayenne gut-reboot kombucha
- Elderflower immunity kombucha
- Kombucha brewed by a guy named Sky who also plays the banjo in an acoustic folk trio

There are flavors so mystical, they just say *"earth"* on the label.

You drink it anyway. It's probably good for your soul.

Local Produce That Glows

Thanks to the rain and volcanic soil, the **fruits and veggies here are thriving.**

You'll find:

- Apples that practically sparkle
- Berries that taste like summer nostalgia
- Kale so fresh it could vote
- Mushrooms foraged by people with podcasts

And don't even start on the **stone-ground, hand-milled, low-impact, wild yeast sourdough bread.**

You'll cry.

Organic? That's the Minimum.

This isn't just the land of organic.

This is the land of:

- Certified humane
- Locally sourced
- Carbon-neutral
- Plastic-free
- Regenerative
- "Made using solar energy and good intentions"

Shoppers carry **cloth bags**, **compostable produce bags**, and **judgment** for anyone reaching for the plastic.

Seafood Aisle = Epic

Being right on the coast means the seafood is *ridiculous*:

- Wild-caught salmon
- Dungeness crab
- Steelhead trout
- Oysters with tasting notes like wine (*"briny with a hint of sea poem"*)
- And sushi rolls prepped fresh with actual respect

Bonus: You can buy smoked salmon as a **snack.** Because why not?

Final Thought

In Washington, grocery shopping feels like a gentle reminder to **live better, buy smarter, and hydrate with intention.**

If your cart contains wild blueberries, lavender kombucha, four kinds of kale, and a coffee made by monks in the mountains?

Welcome to the Evergreen State.

CHAPTER 26

TENNESSEE – HOT CHICKEN, HOTTER SAUCE & GROCERY SOUL

Tennessee is a slow drawl, a fast guitar solo, and a plate of food that makes you forget your phone.

This is where grocery shopping is part concert, part cookout, and always **just a little bit spicy.**

If your cart doesn't hum with soul by the time you leave, **go back in. You missed something.**

Aisle 5: The Hot Chicken Hall of Fame

If it says *"Nashville-style"* on the label, **brace yourself.**

The hot chicken legacy lives on in:

- Frozen hot chicken strips
- Hot chicken dip
- Hot chicken-flavored chips

- Hot chicken *scented* air fresheners (okay... not yet, but we're close)

And of course:

Bottled sauces with names like *"Reckless Heat"* or *"Bless Yo' Mouth."*

Because here, **heat is an identity.**

Southern Sauces & Sunday Sides

Tennessee grocery stores know the secret to a good meal:

It's all in the sides.

You'll find:

- Collard greens with bacon already mixed in
- Mac and cheese with four cheeses and zero shame
- Mashed potatoes you only have to heat—but everyone will still compliment
- Gravy mixes with more history than your cousin's banjo

And sauces? Don't even play:

- White BBQ
- Vinegar BBQ
- Spicy peach glaze
- And "secret sauce" that comes with zero explanation and all the flavor

The Biscuit Section Is Personal

Biscuit mix gets **top shelf treatment** here.

And the refrigerated dough section?

A battleground of brand loyalty.

You'll see:

- Flaky biscuits
- Buttermilk biscuits
- Cheddar biscuits
- Biscuits that come with their own sausage gravy

And if you're not buying biscuit mix named after someone's great-grandma, are you even shopping?

Live Music Energy, Even in Frozen Foods

Even the frozen meals **feel country.**

There's:

- Chicken-fried steak
- Cornbread dressing
- Pulled pork mac and cheese
- Cinnamon swirl French toast casserole
- And banana pudding *with Nilla Wafers included, thank you very much*

These aren't TV dinners.

They're **front porch dinners.**

Gospel, Grits, and Grocery Aisles

You might hear gospel playing overhead.

You'll definitely hear someone say *"How's your mama?"*

And you might get into a friendly debate about cornbread recipes near the baking aisle.

That's Tennessee.

Final Thought

In Tennessee, food isn't just eaten—it's **sung about**, **shared**, and **remembered.**

If your grocery cart holds hot sauce, biscuit mix, greens, banana pudding, and something fried that wasn't on your list...

You're in the right place.

CHAPTER 27

NEBRASKA–FLATLANDS, FULL CARTS & CASSEROLE COMMITMENTS

N ebraska is often called "flyover country," but that's because people don't realize: **there's magic in the margins.**

Especially in the grocery store, where community, comfort, and casseroles quietly hold the state together.

If you're lucky, you'll leave the store with a cart full of practical brilliance—and maybe a pie from someone's church.

Aisle 6: The Cream of Something Section

You know you're in Nebraska when there's:

- Cream of mushroom
- Cream of chicken
- Cream of celery

- Cream of "we're not sure, but trust us, it makes the casserole better"

This aisle is **the backbone of every potluck** from Omaha to a cornfield near nowhere.

Bonus: You'll also find French-fried onions, crushed crackers, and the sacred bag of shredded cheese that's always on sale.

Casserole Culture

Nebraska doesn't just eat casseroles.

They live by them.

You'll see frozen options with names like:

- "Harvest Bake"
- "Country Chicken Delight"
- "Three-Bean Twist"
- "Beefy Noodle Hug" (okay that one might've been mine)

And somewhere near the frozen peas is a whole shelf labeled simply:

"Family Size."

Steady Snacks, Solid Choices

This is not the place for wild snacks shaped like dragons.

This is the place for:

- Cracker assortments
- Sharp cheddar cubes
- Summer sausage
- A surprisingly excellent trail mix section
- And at least one thing involving ranch seasoning, because **of course**

Also: popcorn. Lots of it.

Nebraska is one of the top popcorn producers in the country—and they *don't* mess around.

Meat and Potatoes: The Eternal Combo

The butcher counter is calm, confident, and **absolutely reliable.**

You'll find:

- Roasts
- Pork chops
- Hamburger patties as thick as your winter boots
- And stew meat packaged for slow cookers *that haven't missed a Sunday in 10 years*

And don't forget the **five-pound potato sacks**—bought without question, because *they'll get used.*

Polite Prices & Politer People

People here grocery shop like they drive—**steady, friendly, and not trying to cut you off.**

Expect:

- Smiles at the checkout
- Someone offering to help load your car
- And possibly a small child telling you their family's entire recipe for cornbread

Because in Nebraska, food is **how we care.**

Final Thought

Nebraska grocery stores aren't loud, trendy, or trying to go viral.

They're warm. They're wise. They're **built for real life.**

And if your cart includes cream of something soup, frozen corn, mild cheddar, and something with the word "delight" on the label?

You're right where you need to be.

CHAPTER 28

INDIANA–JELLO PRIDE & FAIRGROUND FLAVOR

ndiana is humble, hearty, and always **ready to feed a crowd**.

It's the kind of place where your grocery cart isn't about personal indulgence—it's about making sure **everybody gets seconds**.

If you're not leaving with a tray of something baked, battered, or buttered...

You'll probably get a *"You okay, hon?"* from the cashier.

Aisle 2: Jello. All Day.

Let's just say it: **Indiana is a gelatin-forward state.**

You'll find:

- Lime jello

- Cherry jello
- Orange jello with floating mystery fruit
- "Party packs" of gelatin powder so big you could hold a wedding reception in it
- And pre-made jello cups with whipped topping already included—*bless.*

There's also *"salad jello,"* which includes things like shredded carrots and marshmallows.

We don't question it.

We respect it.

The Deep-Fried Section Is a Vibe

Indiana lives for fair food. And even when it's not fair season, grocery stores lean into the flavor.

In the freezer:

- Corn dogs
- Fried pickles
- Funnel cake kits
- Mini elephant ears
- Deep-fried mac and cheese balls that come with dipping sauce and dreams

Even the cheese sticks here have *ambition.*

Meat + Noodles = Comfort Math

Casseroles are Indiana's **love language.**

And the key formula is:

- Some meat
- Some noodles
- A cream-of-something binder
- Topped with shredded cheese or fried onions, *or both if you're emotionally generous*

You'll see entire endcaps of:

- Egg noodles
- Cream of chicken soup
- Pre-shredded cheddar
- And pie crusts, because **you might as well finish strong**

Snack Table Royalty

Indiana grocery stores stock up for:

- Church gatherings
- Family reunions
- Euchre night
- "Just in case someone stops by" occasions

So the snacks are **strategic**:

- Cheese cubes
- Little Smokies

- Pickles on toothpicks
- Crockpot liners
- Ranch seasoning packets (plural)
- Velveeta bricks stored like gold bars

And of course: a "family size" bag of chips that *isn't actually enough.*

Politeness at the Checkout, Always

People will chat.

People will compliment your casserole decisions.

Someone will say, *"That's the good brand of pie crust, nice choice."*

Because in Indiana, grocery shopping is **personal, communal, and gently competitive** (especially around the holidays).

Final Thought

In Indiana, your grocery cart isn't about flash.

It's about **feeding people, warming hearts, and maybe winning best dish at the potluck.**

If your cart holds egg noodles, cream of chicken soup, cheddar cheese, and one pack of lime jello...

You're ready for whatever gathering life throws at you.

CHAPTER 29

MISSISSIPPI–BUTTER, BISCUITS & BLESS-YOUR-HEART BARGAINS

Mississippi doesn't just do flavor—it does **soul.** It's the kind of place where recipes are passed down by memory, not measurements.

Where the grocery store smells like cornbread and quiet confidence.

And yes—**everything tastes better with butter.**

(Most of it was cooked in it anyway.)

Aisle 1: Biscuit Territory

In Mississippi, the biscuit section deserves a **moment of silence**.

You'll see:

- Self-rising flour with names like "Dixie Gold"

- Cast iron pans next to the biscuit mix
- Buttermilk biscuits, frozen and fresh
- Canned biscuits for emergencies (we don't judge— *but we notice*)
- And that magical jar of bacon grease sitting next to someone's cart... probably for biscuits

Pro tip: If you buy the wrong biscuit mix, someone's grandmother *will feel it in her knees.*

The Sacred Butter Aisle

There's butter.

Then there's **Mississippi butter.**

You'll find:

- Salted, unsalted, cultured, whipped
- Butter sticks wrapped like Christmas presents
- Butter-flavored shortening (yes, it's a thing)
- "Cooking butter," "table butter," "baking butter," and *"mind your business butter"*

If it can be fried, seared, sautéed, or baked—it was probably introduced to butter first.

Soul Food Staples, Right Where You Expect Them

Walk through a Mississippi grocery store and find the whole story of the South in three aisles:

- Black-eyed peas
- Collard greens (fresh, canned, AND frozen)
- Cornmeal (yellow, white, stone-ground, and pre-blessed)
- Smoked turkey legs in the freezer section
- Hot sauce that ranges from "mild kick" to *"you may see Jesus"*

And don't forget the ham hocks.

They're not for decoration—they're **the secret weapon.**

Cakes, Cobblers & Comebacks

The dessert section is stacked.

Because Mississippi *believes* in sweets that feel like hugs.

You'll see:

- Boxed cake mixes with soul-food remix instructions written on the back
- Peach cobbler kits with canned filling and pride
- Sweet potato pies next to banana pudding bowls
- Evaporated milk, vanilla wafers, and nutmeg lined up like a **flavor choir**

And if you ask someone which dessert is best?

They'll just say, *"Well, it depends who made it."*

Checkout Chat & Cart Etiquette

Southern grocery store lines are **conversations.**

Expect:

- Compliments on your peach selection
- Someone recommending their aunt's cornbread secret (hint: it's mayo)
- A child holding up the line because they can't choose between candy and chocolate milk—and *everyone waits patiently*

Because in Mississippi, grocery shopping is **not a race— it's a ritual.**

Final Thought

In Mississippi, groceries don't just fill your fridge—they **fill your spirit.**

If your cart holds biscuits, black-eyed peas, butter, cornbread mix, and a dessert someone's going to "forget their diet for"...

You're not just shopping. You're feeding generations.

CHAPTER 30

KANSAS–STORM-PROOF STEWS & PRAIRIE PANTRY POWER

K ansas is calm, collected, and always prepared.

Here, grocery shopping is done with **quiet intention** and just a touch of weather paranoia.

Because whether you're feeding the family, the neighbors, or everyone who shows up after a tornado warning, **the pantry better be ready.**

Aisle 5: The Tornado-Ready Essentials

In Kansas, the top five grocery items could power a town:

- Canned chili
- Dry pasta
- Peanut butter
- Boxed cornbread mix
- And a *giant* jug of iced tea

No one panics.

They just stock up and **ride it out with carbs and confidence.**

The Great Midwestern Casserole Belt

Casseroles in Kansas come with unspoken rules:

1. **Always include a starch.**
2. **Cheese goes on top.**
3. **If it feeds less than 8, it's a side dish.**

So the grocery store shows up accordingly:

- Egg noodles by the pound
- Cans of cream soup stacked like bricks
- Bags of shredded cheddar sold in "just in case the cousins visit" size
- Tater tots as topping, filler, and emotional support

You won't find a "Casserole Aisle," but every aisle secretly *is* the casserole aisle.

Meat & Potatoes, Faithfully

The butcher section has one message:

"Let's get through the week."

You'll see:

- Beef roasts

- Ground turkey
- Pork shoulder
- Kielbasa
- And pre-cubed stew meat in family packs

Beside it?

Bags of potatoes like sandbags. Russet, red, Yukon—if it can be roasted or mashed, it's on the list.

Practical Snacks & Prairie Pride

No one in Kansas is buying wasabi kale chips.

They're reaching for:

- Cheese crackers
- Trail mix (hold the exotic stuff)
- Popcorn
- Dill pickles
- Ranch dressing in *bulk,* because everything is a dipping opportunity

Bonus: Kansas shoppers have **deep-rooted cracker loyalty.** You'll find out if you bring the wrong brand to the church potluck.

The Checkout Line Forecast

Someone will mention the weather.

Someone will comment on your bread selection.

And someone will say, *"Supposed to be windy this weekend,"* like that's news.

If you're new in town, this is how they get to know you.

Through **your groceries and your grip on local storm strategy.**

Final Thought

In Kansas, grocery shopping is **no-nonsense, no-fuss, and full of quiet wisdom.**

If your cart has stew meat, potatoes, cornbread mix, a block of cheddar, and something that says *"just in case,"*

You're officially grounded in the Great Plains.

CHAPTER 31

RHODE ISLAND – SMALL STATE, BIG TASTE, COFFEE MILK NATION

R hode Island may be tiny, but it punches way above its grocery weight class.

This state is *bold, briny, and beautifully weird*—and the aisles are full of **regional flex.**

From seafood surprises to snacks that have no business tasting this good, **shopping here feels personal.**

Aisle 3: Coffee Milk Is a Personality

You walk into the dairy section expecting the usual: whole, skim, oat, almond.

And then boom—**coffee milk.**

It's not iced coffee.

It's not a latte.

It's **milk with coffee syrup**, and yes, it's a thing. A very serious thing.

There's even a state law saying **coffee milk is the official state drink.**

You will be judged if you don't at least try it.

(And spoiler: it's oddly addictive.)

The Clam Cake & Chowder Situation

Rhode Island grocery stores have a **regional seafood confidence** that borders on legendary.

You'll find:

- Chowder kits (white, clear, and "don't you dare call it New England-style")
- Frozen clam cakes that somehow still taste like summer
- Quahogs. Yes. Real ones.
- And hot sauce brands you've never heard of but will instantly love

Also: **stuffies** (stuffed clams) that deserve their own national holiday.

Portuguese Rolls & Sausage Goals

The Portuguese influence runs deep in Rhode Island's grocery scene.

You'll see:

- Chouriço sausage (smoky, spicy, glorious)
- Sweet bread that melts in your mouth
- Linguiça, mild or hot
- And Portuguese muffins that look like English muffins but **taste like your life is getting better**

Pro tip: if you see something labeled *"family bakery – Fall River or Pawtucket,"* just buy it. Don't ask questions.

Snacks With Sass

The snack game is small but **mighty**:

- Autocrat coffee syrup (for your milk, your pancakes, or your identity)
- Del's Lemonade frozen pops
- Hot wiener kits (yes, *Rhode Island hot wieners* are a thing—Google it, but not at work)
- And cabinets. Not furniture—milkshakes.
- *(Because why not confuse tourists?)*

Local Loyalty Runs Deep

In Rhode Island, grocery carts are curated with pride.

The cashier might say:

- "Good brand."
- "My uncle works at that bakery."
- "Ooh, haven't had these clam cakes since the 4th of July."

Translation? You're doing it right.

Final Thought

Rhode Island groceries aren't about quantity—they're about **fierce, flavorful identity.**

If your cart includes coffee milk, clam cakes, chouriço, and something your neighbor's Nonna made once and you've been chasing ever since...

You're part of the Ocean State family now.

CHAPTER 32

OKLAHOMA-FRIED BOLOGNA & COWBOY COMFORT

O klahoma is rugged, rooted, and **always ready to feed a crowd.**

It's where you'll find biscuits big enough to block the wind and gravy thick enough to hold a conversation.

The grocery stores here reflect the land: **strong, unpretentious, and full of flavor.**

Aisle 1: Fried Bologna Capital of the World

You haven't truly lived until you've had **fried bologna** in Oklahoma.

The deli section knows:

- Thick-cut bologna? Check.
- Bologna with jalapeños? Absolutely.

- Bologna made locally and wrapped in pride? Of course.
- "Bologna Ends & Pieces" in bulk? You bet.

Add white bread, yellow mustard, a hot skillet, and *childhood unlocked.*

The Meat Section Deserves a Cowboy Hat

Oklahoma is beef country. Grocery stores act accordingly.

Expect:

- Ribeyes thick enough to use as paperweights
- Brisket in sizes labeled "Family" and "County"
- Ground beef bundles that could fuel a chuckwagon
- And sausage links named after someone's uncle (and *rightfully so*)

Don't sleep on the **smoked meats**, either.

There's a section that just *smells like Saturday football and honor.*

Cornbread, Beans & Country Survival Kits

Somewhere near the baking aisle, you'll find:

- Cast iron cornbread pans
- Cornmeal in sacks the size of pillowcases
- Pinto beans by the pound

- Pickled jalapeños in gallon jars
- And hot sauce with names like *"Wrangler Tears"*

This is not "meal prep."

This is **cook-for-20-on-a-Wednesday** energy.

Gravy, Gravy, and Also... Gravy

Flour? Check.

Pan drippings? Check.

Milk? *Don't you dare forget it.*

You'll find:

- Biscuit gravy mix
- Sausage gravy starter
- Turkey gravy packets (even in July)
- And at least one person in the store who says, *"I don't use mix, I just eyeball it."*

Oklahomans don't fear fat. They **honor it.**

The Snack Section Wears Boots

Oklahoma snacks are:

- Bold
- Salty
- Slightly spicy

- Possibly fried

You'll see:

- Pork rinds (in regular, BBQ, and "aggressively seasoned")
- Trail mix with more M&M's than trail
- Jerky made from everything but regrets
- And "Texas Toothpicks" (deep-fried jalapeño slivers) that may or may not start a fire in your soul

Final Thought

In Oklahoma, grocery shopping feels like stocking the pantry for a family reunion you didn't plan—but **you're ready for anyway.**

If your cart has brisket, beans, cornbread mix, bologna, and something with gravy on the label?

You've got Sooner State soul.

CHAPTER 33

COLORADO–ALTITUDE SNACKS & PEAK PERFORMANCE AISLES

C olorado is nature's playground—and the grocery stores are **stocked for the climb.**

Every aisle feels like it's whispering: *"You got this. But make sure it's organic."*

It's a beautiful mashup of outdoorsy practicality, Boulder bougie, and **Denver "I-run-marathons-and-smoke-weed" charm.**

Aisle 4: Trail Mix Royalty

Trail mix isn't a snack here—it's a **nutritional philosophy.**

You'll find:

- Salted, unsalted, deluxe, paleo, keto, gluten-free, nut-free, joy-enhanced

- Mixes with dried mango, cacao nibs, coconut flakes, espresso beans
- Trail mix labeled things like "Summit Fuel" or "Yogi Crunch"
- And DIY bins for **custom mixologists** (aka: you with a scoop)

Pro tip: If it's under $9 a pound, *it's not the good stuff.*

Granola with a Résumé

Granola in Colorado has credentials.

Like, full-on LinkedIn pages.

You'll see:

- Sprouted oat granola
- Hemp seed granola
- Gluten-free alpine vanilla granola baked at 9,000 ft
- Granola made by someone named River who lives in a geodesic dome

It costs $11. You buy it anyway.

It smells like campfire and enlightenment.

CBD in Every Corner

Colorado is **calm.**

Because **CBD is everywhere.**

x

We're talkin':

- CBD gummies
- CBD seltzer
- CBD peanut butter
- CBD dog biscuits
- CBD bath bombs *next to* chamomile tea—**because synergy**

There's even kombucha with CBD in it.

Is it chill?

Yes.

Is it weird?

Also yes.

Does it work?

Honestly... who cares? You feel relaxed just holding it.

Produce That Feels Like It Hiked Here

The fruits and veggies look like they've **trained for this.**

You'll see:

- Apples from local orchards at "elevation-grown" prices
- Carrots with dirt still on them—respect
- Kale so firm it could do a plank
- Beets, turnips, chard, and microgreens with names like "Sunburst Ruby Mix"

And every other label says:

"Grown with snowmelt, compost, and a positive mindset."

Frozen Food for Adventurers

You know what's in the freezer section?

- Organic burritos with 18g of protein
- Gluten-free veggie enchiladas
- "Recovery smoothies"
- Waffle fries for post-ski snack attacks
- And something called *"alt-meat stew,"* which is either vegan chili or an edible TED Talk

Final Thought

In Colorado, grocery shopping is less about impulse and more about **intentional fuel.**

If your cart includes local honey, CBD tea, probiotic yogurt, endurance trail mix, and something fermented?

You're altitude-ready, flavor-focused, and grocery-aligned.

CHAPTER 34

MAINE – LOBSTER ROLLS, FLANNEL VIBES & COLD-WEATHER CARTS

Maine isn't loud.

It's **stoic, scenic, and secretly packing serious grocery game.**

This is a place where lobster rolls live next to baked beans and every cart whispers, *"We survive winters around here."*

The stores are simple, cozy, and totally unapologetic about stocking **four brands of maple syrup next to the chainsaw oil.**

Aisle 3: Lobster, Obviously

Yes.

Lobster.

In grocery stores.

And not in the *"look what we imported"* way—but in the *"my cousin caught that yesterday"* way.

You'll find:

- Live lobster tanks, bubbling quietly in the back
- Lobster meat pre-picked and ready for your roll
- Lobster bisque
- Lobster ravioli
- Lobster mac & cheese frozen meals (aka: survival joy)

It's not flashy—it's **functional seafood luxury.**

Maple Syrup Like Religion

Maine doesn't *just* do syrup. It **perfects it.**

Expect:

- Fancy-grade, dark amber, and "sugared over a wood stove by a guy named Dale"
- Bottles shaped like trees, leaves, cabins, and flasks
- Syrup you heat before pouring because *of course*
- And a stern warning: **"That pancake syrup from the big brands? No."**

Baked Beans, Brown Bread & Granite-Solid Groceries

Mainers love their **traditions**:

- B&M Baked Beans (canned, but blessed)
- Brown bread in a can—don't ask, just toast it
- Whoopie pies the size of softballs
- Red hot dogs (called *"snappers"*)
- And blueberry everything—from jams to pies to pancake mix to soap

If you don't leave the store with something blueberry-flavored, **the state might revoke your visit.**

Frozen Foods for Blizzard Days

Maine freezers are **war-ready.**

You'll see:

- Chicken pot pies as thick as tree stumps
- Ice cream even in January (because *Mainers don't back down*)
- Shepherd's pie
- Chowders in microwaveable tubs
- And frozen bread dough ready to rise if you're snowed in for six days

This is **grocery prep with granite grit.**

People Don't Talk Much—But Their Carts Speak Volumes

Maine grocery shopping is quiet, calm, and practical.

No cart rage. No chaos. Just...

- Flannel-clad humans
- A lot of canned goods
- A quiet nod of approval at your butter selection

Because here, your cart doesn't say "trendy."

It says **"prepared."**

Final Thought

In Maine, groceries reflect the land: rugged, honest, and full of **unexpected comfort.**

If your cart holds baked beans, maple syrup, a sack of potatoes, and something blueberry?

You've earned your place at the flannel-covered table.

CHAPTER 35

ARKANSAS–GRAVY, GRITS & GROCERY GOSPEL

Arkansas is warm, proud, and unfussy.

It doesn't need to shout—**its food does that for it.**

Here, the grocery store is where Southern staples meet Delta soul, and where your cart might include everything for a fish fry *and* a family reunion—because honestly, they're probably the same thing.

Aisle 5: Fried & Blessed

Arkansas doesn't fear frying.

It *honors* it.

In grocery stores, you'll find:

- Cornmeal mix stacked like sandbags

- Fish fry kits with spice blends passed down like scripture
- Hot sauce with names like *"Cousin Clyde's Caution"*
- And catfish fillets—frozen or fresh—waiting for their deep-fried destiny

And right nearby:

Hushpuppy mix. Because no fish should swim alone.

Gravy Gets Its Own Category

Arkansas has a *gravy economy.*

You'll see:

- Sausage gravy packets
- Peppered white gravy in jars
- Bacon grease sold **on purpose**
- Mixes with instructions like *"just add soul"*

This is not a garnish. This is **gravy as foundation.**

Pour it on biscuits, potatoes, meatloaf, eggs, toast... and feelings.

Biscuits Bigger Than Ambitions

Biscuits in Arkansas are a way of life.

In the store you'll find:

- Frozen buttermilk biscuits that rise like *prayers answered*
- Canned ones for weeknights
- Flour blends labeled "Mama's Mix"
- And butter? Oh, honey. **Real, salted, golden.**
- (If your cart has margarine in it, the store might issue a warning.)

Southern Staples Aisle (Unlabeled but Obvious)

You'll know it when you see it. It includes:

- Collard greens in cans and bags
- Black-eyed peas
- Pork shoulder, neck bones, and fatback
- Jiffy cornbread mix
- Sweet pickles and pepper jelly
- And Kool-Aid packets in enough flavors to start a paint store

There's also likely a display of **banana pudding kits**, complete with wafers and instant vanilla pudding *blessed by angels.*

Carts with Soul & Sauce

People in Arkansas shop with intention.

You're likely to see:

- A gallon of sweet tea
- A BBQ sauce that has won *at least one county fair*
- Pie crusts and fruit filling next to a handwritten recipe taped to the shelf
- And a "Family Size" label on **literally everything**

Don't forget:

If someone has three kinds of relish in their cart—they're probably hosting.

Final Thought

In Arkansas, the grocery store isn't flashy—it's **faithful.**

It's stocked for Sundays, storms, supper, and second helpings.

If your cart holds cornbread, catfish, Kool-Aid, butter, and biscuits...

You're shopping like a true Arkansan.

CHAPTER 36

WEST VIRGINIA – PEPPERONI ROLLS, PINTO BEANS & MOUNTAIN CART MAGIC

West Virginia doesn't do flashy.

It does **real.**

Real food, real people, real carts built for both Sunday supper *and* deer season.

The grocery aisles here feel like a mix between your grandma's pantry and a mountain lodge—**hearty, humble, and ready for anything.**

Aisle 1: Pepperoni Rolls Are a Grocery Right

Let's be clear: **pepperoni rolls are sacred.**

These aren't just snacks—they're **portable, greasy bundles of joy** born in the coal mines and baked into the soul of the state.

In every store you'll find:

- Bakery-fresh pepperoni rolls (sometimes warm)
- Bagged versions near the bread aisle
- Pre-sliced ones for lunchboxes
- Frozen ones for emergencies (and yes, *they count*)
- Even gluten-free attempts (we support the effort)

Want to spark a debate? Ask who makes the best one.
Then step back.

Beans & Cornbread: The Holy Combo

This state takes comfort food seriously.

No frills—just **flavor and legacy.**

Grocery essentials include:

- Dried pinto beans in ten-pound sacks
- Cornmeal mix (white, yellow, and "Appalachian stone ground")
- Fatback and ham hocks for flavoring
- Hot sauce with a vinegary snap
- And big white onions—*because pinto beans don't work without them*

Some stores even stock **cast iron skillets** nearby.

Why? *Because they get it.*

Deer Season = Cart Shift

Around mid-fall, grocery shopping gets... tactical.

You'll see:

- Butcher paper rolls by the checkout
- Camo everything
- Freezer bags the size of pillowcases
- Meat tenderizer kits
- Cans of creamed soups *specifically for post-hunt casseroles*

Even the soda deals say things like:

"Stock up before the big buck drops."

The Appalachian Snack Scene

West Virginians snack with purpose:

- Pickled eggs in a jar
- Slim Jims in bulk
- Dill-flavored everything
- Cheese puffs bigger than your head
- "Faygo, RC Cola, or bust" soda energy
- And always, *always* a Little Debbie cake of some kind

No one leaves the store without a snack that crackles when you open it.

Frozen Section = Survival & Sweetness

You'll find:

- Salisbury steak dinners
- Chicken pot pie
- Frozen dumplings (*for real chicken & dumplings, not shortcuts*)
- Ice cream tubs that say *"Family Size"* but challenge that concept

Also: lots of **fruit cobbler starters.**

Because if you don't leave with something peachy and sugary, did you even shop?

Final Thought

In West Virginia, the grocery cart isn't curated—it's *carved from tradition.*

Every item is rooted in purpose, comfort, or mountain memory.

If your cart holds pepperoni rolls, pinto beans, cornbread mix, hot sauce, and a snack cake that tastes like your childhood...

You're grocery shopping with Appalachian soul.

CHAPTER 37

SOUTH DAKOTA–BISON, BEANS & BIG-HEARTED BUGGIES

S outh Dakota isn't flashy—but it's fierce in its flavor. This is where people stock up like snow is coming (because it probably is), and where food isn't about show—it's about **staying fed, warm, and full of purpose.**

It's the kind of place where grocery carts feel like they could fuel a whole town potluck *and* get someone through a winter storm. And they probably will.

Aisle 3: Bison Is the Boss

Step aside, ground beef.

South Dakota loves its **bison**—leaner, richer, and 100% prairie-approved.

In the meat section, you'll spot:

- Ground bison
- Bison jerky (next to cowboy hats and chewing tobacco, probably)
- Bison steaks that say *"grill me and feel powerful"*
- And sometimes, **bison hot dogs** that taste like history with mustard

This is meat with a story. A strong, silent story.

Beans, Bread, and Blizzard Prep

Grocery stores here are built for **survival—with flavor.**

You'll find:

- Baked beans, refried beans, pinto beans, and "ranch-style" beans
- Fry bread mix (especially in reservation-side towns)
- Chili kits with everything but the weather warning
- Cornbread in boxes labeled "Midwest Gold" or something equally cozy
- And powdered milk, powdered potatoes, powdered *everything*—because you *just never know*

Shopping here is like winter camping, but in your kitchen.

Casserole Central

This is hotdish country in disguise.

Expect:

- Frozen tater tots stacked in family towers
- Shredded cheese bags bigger than your pillow
- Cream of mushroom soup, cream of chicken, cream of "don't ask just stir"
- Rotini, elbow macaroni, lasagna noodles (all three could show up in the same dish)

Bonus: There's usually a church flyer taped to the soup shelf. Potluck incoming.

Snacks That Understand You

South Dakota snack aisles don't try to impress—they just **deliver.**

Look out for:

- Corn nuts
- Snack mixes with no name but perfect ratios
- Homemade jerky in clear bags stapled at the top (*someone's uncle made it*)
- Caramel puffcorn (*blessed*)
- Giant tubs of cheese balls for "hunting season" (*totally not just for hunting season*)

And of course: **pie filling in every flavor**, because dessert is a grocery right.

Frozen Food Fortress

You haven't seen frozen food until you've seen South Dakota in January.

Expect:

- Meatloaf dinners
- Potatoes in 14 forms
- Pies—apple, cherry, rhubarb, mystery blend
- Giant pizzas for "just in case we snow in"
- And **bulk sausage patties**, because biscuits need armor

Final Thought

In South Dakota, grocery shopping isn't curated—it's **calculated.**

It's about warmth, gathering, and getting through long winters with full plates and fuller hearts.

If your cart holds beans, bison, cheese, tater tots, and a plan for six meals ahead...

You're prairie-perfect.

CHAPTER 38

DELAWARE – CRAB CAKES, CHICKEN & COASTAL CART ENERGY

Delaware is small but **strategic**—like that one quiet kid in school who knew all the test answers and brought the best lunch.

And in the grocery game? It plays to win.

With a little East Coast sass and a lot of Mid-Atlantic flavor, grocery shopping in Delaware feels like **beach day meets backyard BBQ meets weekday survival.**

Aisle 4: Seafood Without Apology

You're never far from the ocean here.

And the stores *know* it.

You'll find:

- Fresh crab meat in tiny, pricey tubs (*but worth it*)

- Pre-formed crab cakes labeled *"restaurant quality"*—and they deliver
- Bags of shrimp ready for the grill
- Clam chowder kits
- Fish fry seasonings with more personality than your ex

And yes, **Old Bay is stocked like ketchup**—because it goes on *everything*.

The Poultry Power Play

Fun fact: **Delaware is #1 in chicken production per square mile.**

So in the meat section, you'll see:

- Chicken thighs, wings, breasts—stacked like bricks
- Whole fryers with "grandma's roast" energy
- Pre-marinated lemon pepper packs
- Chicken sausage in flavors like apple maple or chipotle honey
- And rotisserie chickens that sell out *before lunch*

This is **chicken country** in disguise.

Scrapple: The Loyalty Test

You either love it or you *don't know it yet.*

Delaware is firmly in the *love* camp.

In the fridge section:

- Brick-shaped scrapple loaves
- Local brands like Habbersett or RAPA
- Slices pre-packed for "grab, fry, bless" mornings
- And seasoning blends designed just for *that crisp edge*

Locals don't explain it—they just hand you a slice and say, *"Eat it like you mean it."*

Beach Snacks & Bay Energy

Delaware snack aisles feel like they were packed by someone who lives in flip-flops.

Look for:

- Saltwater taffy in pastel chaos
- Utz crab chip bags (*life-changing*)
- Soft pretzels with mustard that fights back
- Lemonade mix in "boardwalk size" tubs
- Gummy sharks, peach rings, and candy sticks sold in scoop bins

There's also *always* a cooler with pre-made subs labeled "Beach Pack." Trust it.

Deli + Dessert = Sweet and Savory Peace

At the deli counter:

- Chicken salad with grapes
- Mac & cheese with elbow pasta pride
- Potato salad with extra paprika
- Coleslaw that makes you rethink cabbage

And near the checkout?

- Peach pies
- Coffee cakes
- Doughnuts that look store-bought but *taste like handmade heaven*

Final Thought

In Delaware, grocery shopping might seem simple—but it packs **flavor, function, and a little beach breeze.**

If your cart has crab cakes, scrapple, Old Bay chips, lemonade mix, and chicken ready for grilling...

You just nailed the First State flavor code.

CHAPTER 39

ALABAMA – BUTTER, BLESSINGS & BISCUIT CART BRILLIANCE

n Alabama, food isn't just food.

It's a **hug, a history lesson, and a hallelujah**, all wrapped in foil and still warm.

And in the grocery store?

You're not just feeding your family—you're *representing your whole legacy.*

Aisle 1: Biscuits That Built the South

Biscuits in Alabama are more than carbs.

They're **currency.**

In the biscuit section, you'll find:

- Buttermilk biscuit mix (bless)
- Frozen biscuits that puff up like family pride

- Canned biscuits for busy mornings (*still counts*)
- Sausage gravy starters right beside them
- And butter? Oh, sweet soul—**salted, whipped, cultured, churned in heaven**

You don't *choose* biscuits in Alabama.

They choose **you.**

The Collard Green Trifecta

You haven't grocery-shopped right in Alabama unless you grabbed:

- A massive bundle of fresh collard greens
- Smoked turkey necks, fatback, or ham hocks (your flavor base)
- And a bottle of vinegar hot sauce labeled *"Extra Soul"*

Some stores even have **pre-washed collards**. That's called **Southern evolution.**

Bonus: Sweet onions and cornbread are never far from the greens.

Meat Section = Deep South Storytelling

You'll see:

- Pork chops
- Oxtails

- Neck bones
- Chicken thighs in "bulk family love" packs
- Ground beef beside frozen cornbread dressing—
  holiday dinner pending

And in the freezer?

- Pig's feet
- Turkey wings
- Catfish fillets
- Gator tail (yep, occasionally)

It's not exotic here. It's just *Tuesday.*

The Dessert Aisle Knows No Shame

If you're counting calories in Alabama, go to the hardware store.

Because this aisle is about **joy.**

You'll find:

- Pound cake mix (or full pound cakes by the register)
- Banana pudding kits (complete with wafers)
- Sweet potato pie crusts ready to fill
- Cobblers in cans
- Boxed red velvet cake mix with instructions like
  "You already know."

And sometimes... *peach cobbler-flavored ice cream.*

That's a spiritual experience.

Sweet Tea Supplies & Snack Church

The sweet tea starter kit =

- Sugar (yes, *that* much)
- Tea bags (Luzianne, don't argue)
- A giant glass pitcher that says "family reunion"

Nearby, you'll see snacks that show up at:

- Baby showers
- Church homecomings
- Cookouts
- That one cousin's "just because" game night

Pork skins, cheese straws, pecan sandies, and "mystery punch" mixes.

It's not a party—it's a **gatherin'.**

Final Thought

In Alabama, groceries aren't about trends. They're about **testimony.**

They say *"I love you"* in butter and *"you're forgiven"* in peach cobbler.

If your cart holds greens, ham hocks, biscuit mix, sweet tea supplies, and something covered in glaze?

You just shopped like a legend.

CHAPTER 40

MISSOURI–RIBS, RAVIOLI & SHOW-ME SHOPPING SWAGGER

Missouri is where the **South flirts with the Midwest**, and where the grocery cart reflects that glorious fusion.

One part slow-smoked comfort.

One part casserole culture.

One part "we're feeding 10, just in case."

Aisle 3: The BBQ Sauce Situation

Let's not tiptoe around it—**BBQ is a lifestyle here.**

In every Missouri grocery store, you'll find:

- Kansas City-style sauces: sweet, smoky, sticky
- Local BBQ brands with names like *"Big Jim's Rib Wizard"* or *"Pitmaster's Secret"*

- Dry rub packets labeled *"for serious meat only"*
- Racks of ribs shrink-wrapped like treasure
- Pulled pork packs in the deli case for those too busy to smoke (no judgment)

And somewhere near the sauce section:

A cart paused mid-aisle while someone has a **heated debate about tang vs. spice.**

Toasted Ravioli: Grocery Royalty

St. Louis doesn't play when it comes to this hometown hero.

Look for:

- Frozen toasted ravioli in boxes with "authentic" stamped 4 times
- Marinara dipping sauce nearby—because yes, that's how it's done
- Cheese or beef varieties (some stores get wild with spicy fillings)
- Pre-made trays for parties, game nights, or Tuesdays

This snack is like a mozzarella stick and a pasta roll had a crispy baby.

Meat + Cheese = Love Language

Missourians shop like they're planning a block party *just in case.*

You'll spot:

- Summer sausage (sliced, whole, snack stick form—you pick)
- Processed cheese spreads with names like "Sharp," "Extra Sharp," and "Sharpest"
- Brick cheddar
- Party trays you tell yourself are "just in case people stop by"

And if there's no Velveeta in your cart?

Someone may politely hand you one.

Pantry of Champions

This is where the casserole energy kicks in.

Expect:

- Mac & cheese (boxed, frozen, and deluxe kit)
- Cream soups for "base sauce magic"
- Corn, green beans, and French fried onions
- Instant mashed potatoes *and* real ones (because layers)
- Pie crusts and filling on BOGO, because why wouldn't you?

Missourians **shop like they host**—even if it's just for themselves.

The Game Day Snack Matrix

Game day is a *very real* grocery category in Missouri.

Carts include:

- Nacho cheese
- Tortilla chips in bulk
- Beer brats
- BBQ meatballs (frozen or DIY)
- A box of pretzels the size of a toddler
- And cookies labeled *"team spirit"* even if it's for curling

Whether it's the Chiefs, the Cardinals, or a college showdown, the cart gets **sporty real fast.**

Final Thought

In Missouri, grocery shopping is **generous, flavorful, and built for gathering.**

 Whether you're smoking ribs, hosting cousins, or just craving toasted ravioli at 2 a.m.—**the store gets you.**

If your cart has BBQ sauce, cheese spread, toasted ravioli, pulled pork, and the fixings for mac & cheese...

You're shopping Show-Me style—and showing out.

CHAPTER 41

GEORGIA-SWEET TEA, PEACH PRIDE & SOULFUL GROCERY SWAGGER

Georgia isn't just Southern—it's **deep South with depth.**

It's the kind of place where your grocery cart feels like a Sunday plate: something baked, something fried, something green, and *something your grandma would've approved.*

Aisle 2: Sweet Tea Supplies Are Sacred

There are two kinds of people in Georgia:

A. Those who make sweet tea

B. And those who make it wrong

So stores come correct with:

- Gallon jugs of pre-brewed sweet tea

- Bulk sugar (because "a little" is not a thing)
- Family-sized tea bags (Luzianne or bust)
- Lemon slices in the produce aisle, *conveniently near the mint*

Even bottled sweet tea brands have **homegrown rivalries.**

Someone will side-eye your brand, and they *mean it with love.*

Peach Everything, Naturally

You knew this was coming.

- Fresh Georgia peaches (seasonal and sacred)
- Peach jam, peach cobbler mix, peach yogurt
- Peach sweet tea, peach BBQ sauce, peach hot sauce
- And peach pie with a *lattice crust of Southern truth*

If you're new in town, bring a peach dessert to the cookout.

It's an edible handshake.

Soul Food Staples, Aisle by Aisle

Georgia grocery stores know the basics aren't just ingredients—they're **foundations**.

Expect to find:

- Collard greens (fresh, chopped, bagged, canned—choose your journey)
- Fatback, smoked turkey necks, and ham hocks for seasoning
- Cornmeal, Jiffy mix, and flour by the sack
- Hot sauce (with 4 brands minimum)
- Black-eyed peas, okra, and canned turnip greens with *attitude*

The South doesn't cook by accident.

Everything has a purpose—and a little bacon grease.

The Butcher Section = BBQ Dreams

Whether it's backyard grillin' or tailgate-style chillin', **meat matters here.**

Look for:

- Pork shoulder, ribs, and chicken wings in "cookout-sized" trays
- Spicy sausage links and country-style breakfast sausage
- Oxtails and turkey wings, because flavor lives in the bones
- BBQ rubs and sauces with generational swagger

There's usually a freezer full of peach wood chips nearby. Coincidence? Never.

Dessert Section = Generational Talent

You haven't *lived* until you've stared at Georgia's dessert section.

You'll find:

- Sweet potato pies (full size or "grab one for the ride home" size)
- Red velvet cake so moist it should come with a warning
- Banana pudding with Nilla wafers in *correct proportion*
- Cobblers in tins, boxes, and sometimes surprise bakery slices by checkout

Pecans also show up **everywhere**, and it's always the right call.

Final Thought

In Georgia, grocery shopping isn't a chore—it's a **family tradition**, a cultural flex, and a flavorful stroll through legacy.

If your cart holds sweet tea, collard greens, peach jam, smoked meat, and banana pudding...

You're grocery shopping with Georgia soul.

CHAPTER 42

OHIO–BUCKEYES, BRATS & CART-WHEELING COMFORT

O hio is a little bit East Coast, a little bit Midwest, and a whole lot of **"we got this."**

The people are practical, the food is familiar, and the grocery aisles hum with **tailgate spirit and casserole confidence.**

Aisle 1: Buckeye Flavor or Bust

Let's talk Buckeyes—not the tree, the **dessert.**

In every Ohio grocery store, you'll find:

- Chocolate + peanut butter Buckeye candies (*a state treasure*)
- Buckeye cookie kits
- Buckeye-flavored coffee creamers
- Buckeye pies at the bakery (*don't fight it*)

- And Buckeye ice cream with literal candy bits mixed in

These aren't just snacks.

They're **team spirit in edible form.**

Tailgate Cart Essentials

Ohio runs on sports.

 Whether it's high school, college, or the Browns—**game day matters.**

Expect to see:

- Hot dogs, brats, and mettwurst
- Chili supplies (Cincinnati-style? Columbus-style? Let the debates begin)
- Nacho trays with the cheese that never cools
- Buns in bulk, potato chips in even bulkier bulk
- Crockpot liners (because slow cookers *live here*)
- And more soft pretzels than a stadium needs

The cart says: *"We're ready."*

The Casserole Corner

This is where the Midwestern energy kicks in.

You'll find:

- Cream soups (mushroom, chicken, cheddar—you name it)
- Elbow macaroni, tater tots, and frozen hashbrowns
- Pre-shredded cheese in "comfort food quantity"
- French-fried onions by the tub
- Canned green beans, corn, and "vegetable medley" with vibes

You don't call it a casserole here. You call it **a dish**—and it disappears fast.

The Bakery Case That Doesn't Miss

Ohio bakery sections come correct.

You'll see:

- Soft dinner rolls in 12-packs that vanish in minutes
- Peanut butter cookies with fork marks (mandatory)
- Coffee cake with icing drips down the sides
- Pumpkin roll with cream cheese swirl
- And a whole endcap of **Amish-baked bread** that makes you rethink toast forever

Bonus: You might find a display for *"Grandma's Church Bake Sale Starter Kit."* That's just good planning.

Freezer = Meal Prep & Blizzard Prep

In the Ohio freezer section:

- Pizza rolls (*for emergencies and non-emergencies*)
- Frozen mac & cheese that could rival your aunt's
- Lasagna trays built to feed "the team"
- Half a wall of pierogies
- And a whole case of frozen dips, including *Buffalo chicken dip that slaps*

Because when snow hits, the food *better hit harder.*

Final Thought

In Ohio, grocery shopping is about **readiness, realness, and repping your block.**

If your cart holds brats, Buckeyes, buns, bulk chili ingredients, and something your grandma would've called "a nice dessert,"

You've nailed Ohio grocery greatness.

CHAPTER 43

ILLINOIS – DEEP DISH, DELI SWAG & FULL-FLAVORED FUNDAMENTALS

Illinois is layered like its famous pizza:

Urban flavor on top, Midwest comfort in the middle, and a crust of grocery confidence.

Whether you're grabbing dinner in downtown Chicago or stocking up in small-town Peoria, **the grocery store never disappoints.**

Aisle 1: The Deep Dish Devotion

This is not your thin, floppy pizza.

This is **a commitment.**

You'll find:

- Frozen deep dish pizzas that require oven mitts and patience

- Take-and-bake pies with layers of sauce, sausage, and Chicago pride
- Pizza sauce sold in jars labeled "chunky, hearty, unapologetic"
- Italian sausage in bulk form, because one link isn't enough
- And shredded mozzarella bags you could bench press

Some stores even sell **pizza cutters shaped like the Sears Tower.** You love to see it.

Hot Dog Aisle = Very Specific Rules

Chicago-style hot dogs are **a lifestyle**, and the stores cater accordingly.

Expect to find:

- All-beef dogs (*no substitutes*)
- Poppy seed buns (mandatory)
- Neon green relish (don't question it)
- Sport peppers
- Celery salt
- Diced onions, tomatoes, and that essential dill pickle spear

And remember: **no ketchup.**

The grocery store knows.

It doesn't even try to offer you any.

The Deli Section is a Symphony

Illinois delis don't play.

You'll find:

- Sliced pastrami, roast beef, and pepper turkey with pride
- Coleslaw with vinegar zing or creamy swagger
- Giardiniera—pickled perfection for your sandwich or soul
- Potato salads in multiple personality types (classic, mustardy, loaded)
- And Italian beef trays you can reheat at home and feel like a king

Don't forget the rolls. Crusty, chewy, and **built for dipping.**

Snacks That Match the Mood

Illinois snack energy is equal parts **bold and comforting.**

Look for:

- Chicago mix popcorn (cheese + caramel = chaos and joy)
- Italian lemon cookies
- Corn chips *and* cheese puffs—because you're bringing the snack table
- Craft sodas and small-batch root beer

- And chips flavored like *"Chicago Steakhouse"* and *"South Side Heat"*

Snack like nobody's watching—but everyone will want some.

Freezer Section = Football & Family Ready

What you'll see:

- Frozen Italian beef trays
- Tater tot casserole kits
- Party pizzas for quick wins
- Bagel bites *and* pizza rolls (*why choose?*)
- Garlic bread that toasts like a dream
- Pierogies, pot pies, and **Midwest calm in a tray**

If you can't decide what's for dinner, Illinois already picked *all of it.*

Final Thought

In Illinois, grocery shopping is **a meal plan, a memory, and a mood.**

Whether you're feeding family, friends, or the fans coming over Sunday, **this cart shows up big.**

If your cart has deep dish, giardiniera, Italian beef, sweet corn, and something dipped in caramel...

You're grocerying like an Illinoisan.

CHAPTER 44
WYOMING–MEAT, MOUNTAINS & FRONTIER-GRADE GROCERIES

Wyoming doesn't boast.

It **prepares.**

This is a state where people buy in bulk, eat with purpose, and **know their way around a cast iron skillet.**

Grocery stores here are part ranch, part cabin, part "we might not leave the house till Tuesday."

Aisle 4: Meat Is Not a Side

In Wyoming, meat is not just the main course—**it's the star, the script, and the standing ovation.**

You'll find:

- Ribeye steaks in packs that look like saddle blankets

- Elk, bison, and venison—when the season's right or the butcher's connected
- Ground beef in 10-pound bundles marked "Family Use" (*or just a good weekend*)
- Jerky in all forms: bison, beef, turkey, "mystery protein"
- Sausage links that should come with firewood

This isn't fancy. This is **fuel for life at elevation.**

Pantry Staples That Actually Matter

No fluff here. Just:

- Canned chili
- Dry beans
- Evaporated milk
- Powdered mashed potatoes (*don't knock it till it's snowed*)
- Cornbread mix in five-pound sacks
- And a shelf labeled *"Gravy. Just Gravy."*

The cart says: *"We're good for the week. Or the month."*

Frozen Section: The Blizzard Backup Plan

The freezers in Wyoming stores are **built for endurance**.

Expect to see:

- Chicken pot pies (deep dish, double crust)
- Lasagna trays that could feed 12
- Burritos in industrial quantities
- Wild game tamales (yes, really)
- Cinnamon rolls the size of snow boots
- Ice cream—even during winter (because *who's gonna stop you?*)

Snacks with Attitude

Wyoming snack energy is **salty, smoky, and satisfying**.

Look for:

- Trail mix with more beef sticks than raisins
- Crackers that double as soup tools
- Cheese blocks, cheese cubes, and "cheese for melting"
- Pickled eggs in a jar
- Giant tubs of popcorn
- And "campfire marshmallows" so big they come with disclaimers

Most snack purchases answer the question: *"Could I eat this alone in a cabin?"*

And the answer is always yes.

The Checkout Line = Boots, Beards & Bacon

People here shop with **respectful silence** and sturdy carts.

You'll often see:

- Work gloves
- Dog food in 40 lb. bags
- Bacon stacked like gold
- And a little girl in cowboy boots holding cookie dough like it's treasure

There's no judgment.

Just **a nod of approval if your bacon-to-beans ratio checks out.**

Final Thought

In Wyoming, grocery shopping isn't casual.

It's **calculated, calm, and quietly confident.**

If your cart has steak, chili, jerky, potatoes, powdered cocoa, and cornbread…

You're not just shopping. You're living ready.

CHAPTER 45

NORTH CAROLINA – BISCUITS, BBQ & AISLE-BY-AISLE ALLEGIANCE

N orth Carolina doesn't just eat well—it **feels** what it eats.

This is where grocery carts are a story:

One part family recipe, one part football weekend, one part *"don't forget Grandma's favorite brand."*

And no matter where you shop, one thing's true:

You're either East or West BBQ. Pick a side. Stay loyal.

Aisle 2: The BBQ Divide is Real

In the Tar Heel State, BBQ isn't food—it's **identity**.

Grocery stores represent both camps:

- **Eastern-style**: whole hog, vinegar-based, tangy and sharp
- **Lexington (Western)-style**: pork shoulder, tomato-vinegar sauce, a touch sweeter

Expect to find:

- Bottles of both sauces side-by-side
- Pork shoulder roasts in "cookout cut" sizes
- Dry rubs with names like *"Carolina Smoke Magic"*
- And slaw—*both white and red*—because even coleslaw takes sides here

BBQ isn't just on your plate—it's **in your cart's DNA.**

The Biscuit Business

Biscuits in North Carolina come with **standards.**

You'll find:

- Buttermilk biscuit mix
- Frozen biscuits that rise like Southern hymns
- Fluffy, flaky, and *don't-even-think-about-using-margarine*
- Sausage patties, country ham slices, and pimento cheese waiting nearby
- Hot honey and fruit jams with names like "Yonder Berry" and "Mountain Peach"

And a quiet nod from the shopper next to you that says, *"Good pick."*

Grits, Greens & Good Mornings

Staples in a North Carolina grocery cart:

- Quick grits, stone-ground grits, cheese grits—**all of them**
- Collard greens (fresh, frozen, and ready to simmer)
- Bacon drippings in a jar (yes, they sell that)
- Pickled okra, chow chow, and pepper vinegar
- And eggs from a local farm with names like "Happy Hens of Harmony"

Even if you're not making a full breakfast, your cart *thinks you might.*

The Cookout Cart Combo

Cookouts in North Carolina are an **institution**.

Carts tend to include:

- Hamburger buns, hot dog buns, and hushpuppy mix
- Carolina Gold BBQ sauce (a mustardy wildcard)
- Sweet tea in gallon jugs, or the supplies to make your own
- Boiled peanuts in a bag (yes, in the store)
- Banana pudding kits (instant or handmade)

And someone always buys more napkins than needed. It's just good manners.

Snack Aisle = Grandma + Game Day

Look for:

- Pork skins
- Pimento cheese spread
- Cheese straws
- Moon Pies
- Cheerwine (you don't sip it—you *respect* it)
- And pecan pies sold "just in case someone stops by"

There's Southern hospitality in every box.

Final Thought

In North Carolina, grocery shopping isn't about rushing—it's about **honoring taste, tradition, and territory.**

If your cart has BBQ sauce (your kind), grits, collards, biscuits, and banana pudding...

You've shopped with Carolina pride.

CHAPTER 46

MARYLAND – CRAB CAKES, OLD BAY & COASTAL CART SWAGGER

Maryland grocery shopping is a little salty, a little spicy, and **full of coastal character.**

From Baltimore to the Eastern Shore, your cart tells a story of family gatherings, seafood feasts, and seasoning loyalty that runs *deep.*

Aisle 1: The Old Bay Universe

Let's start where everyone in Maryland starts: **Old Bay.**

It's not just a seasoning.

It's a **lifestyle.**

You'll find:

- Old Bay in the spice section
- Old Bay-flavored chips

- Old Bay hot sauce
- Old Bay popcorn
- And *yes*, Old Bay goldfish crackers

They'll probably add it to ice cream next—and honestly, people will try it.

Crab Central

Maryland loves its crabs, and grocery stores respect the obsession.

Expect to find:

- Cans of fresh-picked lump crab meat
- Crab cake mix packets (*or family recipes taped to the can*)
- Crab boil kits with seasoning, lemons, and twine
- Crab-shaped kitchen gadgets (yes, even oven mitts)
- Steamer pots that come with warnings like: *"Feeds 10 or go home."*

Some stores have **a live tank**. It's not decoration—it's **dinner scouting.**

Seafood That Stays Winning

Beyond crabs, the ocean vibes are strong:

- Rockfish fillets
- Shrimp trays labeled *"party size"* (*they mean it*)

- Oyster stew starters
- Scallops with garlic butter marination kits
- And clams, mussels, and seafood stock in multiple moods

Everything here smells like *Sunday with cousins and a grill you can hear from the driveway.*

Cookout Carts, Bay Style

A Maryland cookout isn't complete without:

- Hot dogs and burger patties *next to* crab cake patties
- Coleslaw with celery seed and sass
- Potato rolls (always toasted, always respected)
- Mac & cheese so creamy it needs a seatbelt
- Corn on the cob—*with or without Old Bay*

And *somebody* brings a pound cake in foil that disappears before the main course hits.

The Sweet Side of the Bay

Maryland dessert carts lean *comfort + homemade + just a lil' flex*:

- Smith Island cake (if you know, you KNOW)
- Peach cobbler mix (*because the South whispers here too*)

- Vanilla ice cream with a side of caramel sauce (*it's for the cake... maybe*)
- Fudge from a local creamery
- Cider donuts that taste like fall and home at the same time

And if the bakery has Berger cookies?

Put. Them. In. The. Cart.

Final Thought

In Maryland, grocery shopping is **a tidal rhythm of spice, seafood, and celebration.**

It's a cart that says *"We're hosting something—even if it's just Tuesday."*

If your cart has crab meat, Old Bay, coleslaw, rockfish, and something sweet from the bakery...

You're grocerying with Chesapeake confidence.

CHAPTER 47

VIRGINIA–HAM, HISTORY & CART DUAL CITIZENSHIP

V irginia is *where the South begins and the North starts to slow down.*

This means grocery carts here are equal parts comfort, class, and **"Don't forget the hot sauce AND the almond milk."**

You're just as likely to see heirloom tomatoes as you are country sausage—and that's the charm.

Aisle 1: Ham Runs This State

Virginia doesn't just do ham. It **perfected** it.

At the meat counter:

- Salt-cured country ham that can *bite back*
- Spiral-sliced ham for holidays or *just because*
- Ham biscuits (yes, pre-assembled in bakery trays)

- Virginia ham steaks that go straight in a skillet, no questions asked
- And sometimes, whole hams with a *rope handle*

Ham here is not a topping. It's a **legacy.**

The Biscuit Bracket

Virginia biscuits are **non-negotiable.**

You'll find:

- Buttermilk biscuit mix
- Frozen biscuits ready to puff up like pride
- Pimento cheese and honey butter beside them (*as it should be*)
- Sausage patties with that *"Grandpa got up early to make breakfast"* energy
- And jams labeled "Preserved with Purpose"

Bonus: Look for the mini country store section inside the grocery.

There's probably a biscuit mix there *handwritten by someone named Dot.*

Colonial Meets Contemporary in the Cart

Virginia's carts are beautifully conflicted:

- Grits next to Greek yogurt

- Cornbread mix with a bag of organic arugula
- Smoked turkey necks next to plant-based breakfast patties
- Kombucha beside Cheerwine
- Wine from a local vineyard *and* peach preserves from a roadside stand

This is what happens when Thomas Jefferson meets Trader Joe's.

The Snack Vibe

Look for:

- Boiled peanuts (*yes, even in Northern Virginia*)
- Pork skins in resealable "no judgment" bags
- Smithfield-brand everything
- Fancy kettle corn with rosemary sea salt
- And cookies labeled "Tea Room Style" or "Colonial Charm"
- Also? Moon pies. Because *balance.*

Freezer Energy = Slow Cook & Sweet Tooth

Expect to see:

- Pot pies that feel like they came from a covered bridge
- Mac and cheese in slow-bake tins
- Fruit cobblers with biscuit topping (*chef's kiss*)

- Ice cream with peach, blackberry, or "Chesapeake Crunch" flavors
- And chicken & dumplings with *"Sunday supper approved"* on the box

Final Thought

In Virginia, grocery shopping is **graceful, grounded, and gently hybrid.**

Your cart reflects the past, the present, and the dinner you're about to bless.

If your cart has ham, biscuits, pimento cheese, peach jam, and a bottle of something local…

You're grocery shopping with Virginia elegance.

CHAPTER 48

MICHIGAN – CHERRIES, CONEY DOGS & CART-TOTING GRIT

Michigan's grocery cart is a mix of **heartland hustle and lakehouse leisure.**

It's got *up north practicality, Detroit flavor,* and *Grandma's casserole know-how*—all riding on snow tires.

This is a state that knows how to snack, sip, slow cook, and survive winter **like a champ.**

Aisle 2: The Cherry Kingdom

Michigan doesn't *just grow* cherries.

It **celebrates them.**

In the produce and preserves aisles:

- Tart cherries (fresh, dried, or frozen)
- Cherry pie filling in "bake me now" jars

- Cherry salsa, cherry BBQ sauce, cherry vinaigrette
- Cherry juice labeled "pure Michigan pride"
- And full-blown cherry cobbler kits (*bless*)

Buy one thing with cherries, and the cashier will probably say *"Good choice."*

They mean it.

Coney Dogs = Regional Rivalry in a Bun

The *Detroit vs. Flint Coney debate* is **real.**

So the grocery store stocks for both:

- All-beef hot dogs
- Steamed buns
- Canned chili sauce
- Onions (pre-diced if you're lucky)
- Mustard in the squeeze bottle that's always half-empty in real life

Pro tip: Ask which kind of Coney the butcher prefers.

Be ready for a *spirited discussion.*

Great Lakes Grocery Logic

You'll see items like:

- Whitefish fillets from the Upper Peninsula
- Lake perch breading kits

- Local maple syrup next to pancake mixes that *look like family heirlooms*
- Cheese curds from neighboring Wisconsin (we don't talk about it)
- Blueberry everything—*when cherries take a nap*

And a very good chance you'll stumble across a **free sample of something smoked.**

Midwest Casserole Game, Strong

In Michigan, casseroles are *a love language.*

Expect to find:

- Elbow macaroni, egg noodles, and frozen hash browns
- Canned cream soups (mushroom, chicken, cheddar... all present)
- Tater tots in "multi-meal" bags
- Shredded cheese in **pillowcase portions**
- And that one spice blend labeled *"just enough zip"*

Don't forget the French fried onions. Ever.

Freezer = Cozy Chaos

What's inside:

- Pasties (meat-filled pastry pies from Yooper heaven)
- Ice cream with *fudge ripple pride*

- Pizza rolls *next to* cherry crisp
- "Up North"-branded dinner kits
- And frozen cider donuts, because *you're never out of season*

Bonus: Pop, Not Soda

Say "soda" here and someone might hand you a can of **Vernors** and say,

"Try this instead."

Look for:

- Faygo (Redpop is elite)
- Vernors ginger ale (spicy and healing)
- Locally brewed root beer
- And a six-pack of "don't ask questions, just drink it" mystery flavors

Final Thought

In Michigan, grocery shopping is **grounded, hearty, and just a little nostalgic.**

Every aisle feels like it's prepping you for a road trip, a snowstorm, *or both.*

If your cart has cherries, whitefish, hot dog chili, cheese, and a pie crust waiting for greatness...

You're grocerying with Mitten State mastery.

NEW HAMPSHIRE – MAPLE, FLANNEL & CART-DOWN-BY-THE-CREEK ENERGY

N ew Hampshire doesn't yell about its groceries.

It just stocks up quietly, **with fierce intention**.

This is a place where local means *actually local*, bread comes in brown paper, and maple syrup gets its **own grocery shrine.**

Aisle 1: The Maple Monarchy

This is *the* maple syrup capital.

You'll find:

- Maple syrup in every shade: golden, amber, dark, *"this could raise the dead"*
- Maple candies shaped like leaves
- Maple sugar in crystal form (like fairy dust, but sticky)

- Maple butter (it's a spread and a lifestyle)
- Maple granola, maple bacon, maple popcorn, maple EVERYTHING

Pro tip: *Never reach for "pancake syrup."* That's considered an insult here.

Produce with Purpose

New Hampshire's produce section feels like a **farmstand with heating.**

Look for:

- Apples in heirloom varieties (*with handwritten signs*)
- Potatoes, onions, and root vegetables that *look like they just woke up from the earth*
- Kale and spinach so fresh they snap
- Wild blueberries (small, sweet, and seasonal gold)
- And cider jugs that sweat with anticipation

The fruits here don't brag. They **just taste right.**

Bread, Cheese & Candlelight Vibes

In the bakery and deli sections, expect:

- Crusty loaves of sourdough or oatmeal bread in wax paper
- Sharp cheddar from the next town over

- Creamy goat cheese with herbs and hope
- Cider donuts (fresh, frozen, and forever)
- And maybe a surprise display of *"pie of the week"* from a local baker named Janet

Also nearby: candles, handmade soaps, and apple butter.

Because of course.

Pantry = Prepared, Not Panicked

New Hampshirites shop like they've weathered a few storms (they have).

In the pantry aisles:

- Beans (dried and canned)
- Steel-cut oats in "log cabin" quantities
- Baking supplies for banana bread emergencies
- Tea, honey, and hot cocoa that *feels like a blanket*
- And pasta sauces that say "We might be snowed in, but we're eating well."

The vibe is: calm cart. Full cupboard. Can't lose.

Snack Aisle = Hiker Fuel

These snacks are trail-tested:

- Granola bars with six nuts and a PhD
- Trail mix called *"White Mountain Crunch"*

- Popcorn with sea salt, maple glaze, or cheddar dust
- Dried fruit that could pass as fresh
- Crackers made with rye, oats, flax, and *moral superiority*

Plus, at least three types of jerky.

Because **this state hikes.**

Final Thought

In New Hampshire, grocery shopping is **seasonal, thoughtful, and ruggedly sweet.**

Every item in the cart whispers: *"I've got you through this winter, friend."*

If your cart holds maple syrup, sharp cheddar, cider donuts, root vegetables, and hiker-grade granola...

You're grocerying with Granite State soul.

CHAPTER 50

CONNECTICUT – COASTAL CALM, CIDERFEELS & CART-CLASS IN SESSION

Connecticut grocery shopping is all about **balance**: Seaside meets countryside. Cozy meets classy.

The carts are curated—not because they're trying to impress, but because **Connecticut just shops that way.**

Aisle 1: The Apple Cider Aesthetic

In Connecticut, **fall is a personality**, and the cider aisle proves it.

You'll see:

- Fresh apple cider in glass jugs
- Sparkling cider with gold foil on top (*holiday energy, all year*)
- Cider donuts with actual dustings of sugar, not sprinkles

- Apple butter jars labeled *"Small Batch, Big Flavor"*
- And hard cider in craft cans with minimalist fonts

Fall in this state isn't a season. It's a **flavor profile.**

The Lobster Roll Decision Zone

Connecticut does things *differently*.

While Maine slathers their lobster rolls in mayo, Connecticut keeps it real with:

- Hot, buttered lobster rolls
- Brioche buns or split-top rolls toasted to perfection
- Seafood salad kits that say *"just heat and assemble"*
- Pre-cooked lobster meat in "weekend treat" packaging
- And drawn butter in cute containers with an identity crisis (sauce or dip? Yes.)

Pair it with kettle-cooked chips and a lemon wedge.

Instant seaside serenity.

New England Bakes & Bread Baskets

In the bakery:

- Portuguese rolls, English muffins, ciabatta, multigrain—you name it
- Apple pies, pear tarts, cinnamon swirl loaves

- Cornbread muffins that would hold up at any potluck
- A small stand of *gluten-free, dairy-free, probably joy-filled* pastries
- And scones that whisper "brunch at 10?"

Also nearby: maple syrup (Vermont adjacent, but no less respected) and real butter that's *locally cultured.*

Deli + Cheese = Northeastern Art

Grocery stores here *know their audience.*

You'll find:

- Sharp cheddar, French brie, herbed goat cheese
- Smoked salmon in "bagel brunch portions"
- Deli meats in eco-pack containers
- Hummus labeled with Greek islands
- And fig jam next to truffle oil, because the charcuterie board won the war

You're not just shopping for a sandwich. You're preparing an *experience.*

The Quietly Bougie Snack Aisle

Connecticut snack culture = *subtle luxury*:

- Dark chocolate almonds
- Parmesan crisps
- Pita chips with sea salt and Himalayan vibes

- Artisan popcorn (*with rosemary or white cheddar dust*)
- Local honey sticks and granola clusters named after nearby towns
- And trail mix that includes dried cranberries and exactly four cashews

Some carts also contain *kombucha—but they don't make a big deal about it.*

Final Thought

In Connecticut, grocery shopping is **deliberate, local, and layered with taste.**

Each cart feels like a reflection of the weekend ahead— relaxing, refined, and just a little cozy.

If your cart holds apple cider, lobster rolls, baked goods, fancy cheese, and something subtly sweet...

You've just grocery-shopped your way through Connecticut—and completed all 50 states.

WASHINGTON, DC–SUITS, SNACKS & GROCERY-STATE DIPLOMACY

D C doesn't just shop.

It strategizes.

In the nation's capital, your cart might contain:

- Kale for the committee hearing
- Cold brew for your 12 Zooms
- Cupcakes for the caucus
- Wine for the watchdogs
- And a full charcuterie board "just in case the ambassador stops by"

Every grocery item has **intention**—and possibly a voting record.

Aisle 1: The Global Flavor Index

DC is *international* to its core.

So the stores respond with:

- Aisles labeled "Asian," "Middle Eastern," "Latin," and "East African"
- Gochujang next to harissa next to preserved lemons
- 9 types of rice, 6 kinds of hot sauce, and a corner freezer full of samosas
- Pita, naan, injera, and Ethiopian spice blends in bags labeled "family pack"
- Tofu in diplomatic quantities

You can build an **entire UN potluck** in one trip.

Power Lunch Logistics

Every grocery store has these stocked:

- Pre-packed salads with pomegranate seeds and ambition
- Hummus in "debate-night size"
- Protein bars named after startup founders
- Fancy sparkling water (cucumber mint is just *Tuesday*)
- And cold brew in bulk

Also available: microwaveable quinoa bowls that whisper *"do the work of three interns."*

Bakery + Wine = After-Hours Hill Snacks

Look for:

- Georgetown Cupcakes (*never underestimate their political pull*)
- Lemon bars with an "executive summary" of zest
- Mini cheesecakes labeled *"weekend talking points"*
- Cabernet that reads as "I'm listening"
- Prosecco that says *"I made it through the vote count."*

And a pre-made cheese board labeled *"for important guests or impressive in-laws."*

Snack Aisle Bipartisanship

Where else can you find:

- Vegan BBQ chips and cheddar goldfish side by side
- Seaweed snacks next to Takis
- Granola bars that promise to "fuel your best self"
- Popcorn with nutritional yeast AND "loaded nacho" flavor
- Dark chocolate labeled "90% cacao and 10% policy grit"

It's the one aisle where **everyone reaches across the cart.**

Farmer's Market Vibes on Aisle 7

Even in chain stores, you'll find:

- Local honey from Maryland hives
- Microgreens with names like "Urban Kale Sparkle"
- Organic eggs from Virginia farms
- Jars of jam that look like they went to prep school
- And apples with more degrees than your intern

Shopping here feels like the *food equivalent of C-SPAN: reliable, honest, and occasionally spicy.*

Final Thought

In DC, grocery shopping is part power move, part comfort ritual, and part global village run on espresso.

If your cart has kale, cold brew, global spices, sparkling water, and a box of cupcakes...

You're grocerying with District style.

MORE THAN JUST GROCERIES

S o here we are—at the end of the aisle.

Fifty states and one District of Columbia later, we've seen it all:

 Butter and brisket. Kombucha and cornmeal. Lobster rolls, cheese curds, hot sauce, and sweet tea.

But what this journey really revealed wasn't just what's on the shelves.

It was what's in the hearts of people, in the quirks of communities, in the **quiet ways we live, celebrate, adapt, and remember.**

Because groceries aren't just about food.

They're about:

- The comfort you grab after a long day.
- The flavor that reminds you of home.
- The choices that define your culture—and sometimes your identity.

- The gathering you plan around a dinner table.
- The future you fill your cart for.

And only in America—**this wild, wonderful land of at least 50 options**—could the grocery store become such a rich reflection of everything else we are: diverse, expressive, hilarious, practical, proud.

My hope is that after reading this book, you'll never walk into a grocery store the same way again.

That you'll see a little more story in the soup aisle.

A little more magic in the melons.

A little more *America* in every aisle.

Now go fill your cart.

 Your story's still being written.

— **Robert Okine**

ABOUT THE AUTHOR

Robert Okine is a global nomad, curious soul, and devoted family man who's traveled the world—often with a cart in one hand and a snack in the other. A tech CEO by profession and a storyteller at heart, Robert has spent years exploring different cultures, cuisines, and grocery store habits across continents.

He believes that what we buy, cook, and share says just as much about us as where we live—and nowhere does that show up more hilariously or beautifully than in America's grocery stores.

Now based in Washington, DC (though still frequently on the move), Robert's adventures continue with his wife, Yaanieta, and their two incredible children, Jason and Kaitlyn.

USA: The Land with at Least 50 Options is his debut book—and a love letter to flavor, family, and everyday culture... one shopping cart at a time.